BO

STAY SORE

How to Break Through the Fear of Change into a Better Life

BY

BO SKITSKO

STAY SORE

Ordering Information: Quantity sales. Special discounts are available on quantity purchases by corporations, associations, and others. Orders by U.S. trade bookstores and wholesalers.

www.DreamStartersPublishing.com

Table of Contents

Introduction

Fun fact: I'm writing this introduction after I finished the book. Writing this is actually much harder than the book itself because now I have to introduce myself and explain to you why I am worthy of your attention.

First of all, thank you so much for purchasing this book and investing in yourself. Second, if this book gives you at least one nugget of wisdom, or challenges your thinking patterns in one way or another, then I have already achieved my mission! Because it all starts with your perception, with your thinking and belief patterns, with your ability to create and analyze ideas. It all starts with what your heart and your mind believes to be true.

My name is Bo Skitsko. I am not claiming to have a lot of wisdom or knowledge. But I do believe that I have some experience to share that can potentially help you achieve your fitness and life goals if applied.

I was born in Ukraine and raised in Germany. When I came back to Ukraine, I studied international law for 3 years, and I discovered that this was most certainly not what I wanted to do for the rest of my life. Just before I turned 21, my family and I immigrated to America in pursuit of a better life. It took us "only" 12 years to get all the immigration documents approved legally.

Let's start with Germany. When we moved there, I was two weeks late for the first grade, and all the kids already knew each other. I didn't even speak or understand one word of German. Needless to say, I was an outsider. I was bullied every day mentally and physically. It took me about a year to learn the language, pull myself up and become one of the "cool" kids in school.

When we moved back to Ukraine, I was in the 7th grade. Because I had spent all of my early years in Germany, I couldn't even write in my own native language. All the kids believed that I thought I was better than them, which was not true. So I got bullied again, I was beaten up and made fun of almost every day. It took me a little over a year to pull myself up and to become one of the "cool" kids in school once again.

Then, I immigrated to America as a young adult, I had to take jobs that did not require me to know English because, once again, I did not speak the language of the country I was living in. My first job here was cleaning cheap apartment buildings and toilets. I definitely did not need any language skills for that. My dream was to learn English well enough to be able to have a cashier position at the local Walmart, so I wouldn't have to clean apartments and toilets anymore. But that seemed very unrealistic. So, I tried many different jobs that did not require me to know English. For the next few years, I did construction, hardwood floor installation, delivery driver, mover, and many other things.

To make a very long story short, today is the 10 year anniversary of my American journey. I own my own business, a fitness studio which is called Bo-Fit (BoFit LLC). I provide jobs in the community. I have a degree in exercise science and countless certifications in my respected field because I love to always improve myself. I have a beautiful wife, two healthy boys and one on the way. I am writing this book in a foreign language for me - English. And I can truly say that I am changing lives for a living, which is the best job I can think of!

This book is about change. This book is about achievement and success, in whichever form you choose to perceive success. It is about the fear of change and how to turn it into something positive. This book is called "Stay Sore" because I truly believe that nothing good comes easy. Every time you want to achieve something big, and of significance in your life, you need to get uncomfortable and work hard on it!

Change is never-ending. You can fight it, or you can use it to your advantage. It is time to share my story right here and right now. Therefore I have to just let go and put it in your hands. Enjoy and Stay Sore!

Chapter One

Write it Down!

This might seem an odd way to start out, but trust me when I tell you that it is the most important practice that you can add to your daily life! When you write something down on paper, it comes to life. At the end of the day, we all want something for ourselves that will bring us happiness. We all have dreams and plans, and ideas for getting there. Writing them all down on paper allows us to touch and feel them in more tangible ways and see if we are making any sense. And, when I say write it down, I am talking about good old-fashioned paper and pen or pencil! I am not talking about using a phone or computer, which will fill in the rest of your sentence or autocorrect your "idea." For me, it must be written in ones own hand. Why? Because there is a deeper connection created when you write things out in your own hand. A connection you cannot get or feel when you just type into a word document program or speak words into your phone.

Don't get me wrong. The "notes" app on my phone is filled with ideas for different projects, future social media posts for my business page, and even half of the ideas for this book were created "on the go" by using speech to text on my phone. But when it comes to your goals, things that give your life meaning, those have to be written down on paper in your own handwriting. There is a time for typing, and there is a time for writing. Learn to feel the difference.

Most of what we visualize in our heads, as goals or dreams, is very vaguely represented with a singular thought or idea. By its nature, writing in longhand promotes critical thinking. When you start putting word after word on paper, you start realizing that in order to have a grammatically correct sentence, you need to choose your nouns, pronouns, verbs, and adjectives very carefully. Every word you chose becomes very meaningful and in turn, can change your goal dramatically. This will force you to create a very specific and deeply analyzed goal. Even more so, you will start to realize how big or small your goal actually is.

There have been studies done in colleges that showed students that used laptops to take notes were just typing them verbatim. The result was, although they had typed out the words, they did not process the material. Therefore, they did not score as highly in comprehending the information. Typing the professor's lectures word for word left a very shallow imprint of the information on their brains. This did not allow them to absorb and understand the information within their own frame of mind. The notes that students wrote out in longhand were more acutely processed, becoming embedded in their minds for later recall.

There have also been many studies conducted that show how the function of handwriting is very important for the development of the cognitive area of the brain. That part of the brain that gives us the ability to work with the information we have in a meaningful way. In short, it is how the brain processes and allows us to apply any knowledge we have acquired. I truly believe in this because I know it works for many successful people I have learned from as well as myself.

Sometimes halfway through the process of writing, you might find things are not making sense. When this happens, you need only to take a step back, rethink, and adjust. Say my goal is so huge that what I really need to do is to break it down into smaller bits to make it more manageable. For instance, say I want to start a business. I have an idea of what I want the business to be and maybe even a name for it. But that's all. Well, that is very vague, and I have no idea how I can do this. It seems I am defeated before I even start. What I really need to do now is to keep writing up ideas. It helps me to identify all the steps I will need to take to get me there. In this way, my brain is able to organize and process the smaller bits of information into a path for reaching my final goal. And I will have done it more effectively with fewer mistakes and hassles along the way.

Until I was about 25 or 26 years old, I never sat down and read a book. I never wrote anything down because I was always just winging it. I would have what I call these "genius ideas," but the next day, when I woke up, I couldn't remember them. It was very frustrating! So I started to make small notes for myself, and those thoughts and notes later turned into big ideas; that maybe I should help people for a living, that maybe I should become a personal trainer, that maybe I should start a business, that maybe I should write this very book. That I could do something bigger. I knew that I had the potential. I was willing to put forth the effort and work hard. I just didn't know how to get started and then make it grow.

So, at 26 years old, I started reading books. But I hadn't been able to really feel it and start anything of significance until I read a book by Brian Tracy, "No Excuses. The Power of Discipline". In his book, he talks about writing everything down on paper. Not on a computer or on your phone, but on paper! It made sense to me when I thought about it. So, I started writing. What I found as I put things on paper was that the things that seemed so far in the distance and so unachievable became closer than ever. With each sentence, my goals and plan of action seemed more doable. I ended up with 3 goals for the whole year. One for my business, one for my spiritual growth, and one for my family life. Under each goal, I had 5 to 10 things I needed to do daily in order to achieve them and 5 to 10 things I needed to just get done once – for example, getting an occupancy permit from the city.

I love personal growth! That is why I got the Brian Tracy book and read it. It was that book that lit a spark in me. By nature I am a procrastinator, that's why the title "No Excuses" felt like a big, juicy kick in my behind. And trust me, back then, I needed that kick. Actually, I think we all need that kick once in a while. I was so inspired to start writing everything down. I wrote and wrote and read and re-read my notes. I set goals for myself, goals that would test me. To this day, I can go back to my journal and see exactly where I wrote down my first tangible goals. They gave me a purpose and a reason to move forward in my life. I felt if I accomplished them, I might just be able to start my own business. It was a pivotal moment. One that I could never have predicted.

We can all visualize many things in our heads, but I guarantee that when you write those visions down in longhand on paper, you will see them change and morph into things you hadn't considered. When you write something down, you start to transition the vision in your head into black and white. You start to truly bring your ideas to life and really look at them. Your brain connects the dots and starts to organize and articulate the details as well as the effort and actions needed to make them real. It allows you to see just what it will take to realize your vision or if it even makes sense to move in that direction.

Think about this. When you are handwriting on paper, you have limited distractions. Your focus and attention are directed toward your journaling. It is too easy when you are writing on the computer or with your phone to be distracted by outside forces such as emails or texts coming in. Since we are an instant gratification society, we tend to let ourselves be taken away by these distractions because we must find out what is in that email or text and then answer them right away.

You know what I am saying here is true because I am sure you do it all the time. There is no email or text function attached to a notebook full of paper. Only blank pages waiting for you to spell out your hopes, dreams, desires, and anything else that comes into your mind. It is invaluable to the process of becoming successful and reaching your goals. And it is

PERSONAL. It is you personally conversing with yourself in your own language, and that is MAGIC!

"By recording your dreams and goals on paper, you set in motion the process of becoming the person you most want to be. Put your future in good hands—your own."

Mark Victor Hansen

BO'S HOMEWORK

Go out and get a package of legal-sized tablets.

Place in strategic areas with a pen next to them.

Write, write, write down every thought you have. Goals, dreams, anything that makes your eyes light up.

If you are on the go, type it up in your notes app on your phone.

Watch how your life will begin to change.

NEVER STOP WRITING!

Chapter Two

Set Goals

As you can imagine, my world was filled with anxiety. Here, I had moved my family across continents to bring them to a better place, and I was cleaning toilets. Not exactly what I had thought I would be doing. Every night I was filled with dread and wondering what to do, what to do? I progressed some as my English improved. I transitioned from job to job, growing some each time. But it wasn't enough. I kept on dreaming and writing! My writing kept me focused, and eventually, ideas began to unfold. Ideas that would bring an action. Action is key to soothing anxiety.

Moving along, I transitioned from janitor to delivery driver. From delivery driver to a construction worker and hardwood floor installer. Somewhere in between those jobs, I was also a mechanic. Then I moved on to personal caregiver and finally to part-time trainer. Every time somebody would offer me work and ask me if I knew how to do it, I would just answer "yes" and then stay up all night and actually learn what it is I agreed to. I needed money. I was certified as a trainer by then, but I still couldn't do it full time because of the language barrier. I was reading the study materials for my certification with a dictionary because every third word or so was new to me. I would train my fellow Ukrainian friends and family that spoke the language, but I still couldn't train Americans. I still remember the first check I ever got for being a trainer at a big box gym. It was a whole seven dollars and change! I admit, a bit disappointing. It turned out that personal training isn't so much about the training as it is about selling the training. That's why I only made seven dollars. I didn't realize then that you had to go out on the gym floor and really sell your training skills to make money. I learned it though. As it turned out, I found that I am really good with people. I love to serve others and help them to change their lives and become the best version of themselves. It is my greatest passion to help someone achieve their goals, not just in fitness, but to become the strongest version in all aspects of their lives. This revelation has served me well.

Four years into working full time as a personal trainer and later head trainer of a big fitness center, I finally knew what I wanted to do with my life. I had to be able to help and serve people on my own terms in a way that I believed to be the best, most ethical, and most effective way. This is why I had to open my own gym.

So, I gave myself three months to close a deal with clients outside of the gym where I was working. I figured that I would need a minimum of five clients to get started. They would have to be people who didn't know me, and I was going to have to convince them to work out with me in my less than adequate basement. Okay, it was a real crappy space, with low ceilings and only about 200 square feet of space equipped with equipment that I picked up on Craigslist. We're not talking good stuff here. I'm talking rusty used up equipment. And any person taller than 5 feet could easily reach up and touch the ceiling. This is what it was like when I started out.

I set up these daily and mostly simple goals for myself. One, I had to speak to a minimum of five people every day. Let them know I would be starting a new fitness business in the next year, and I would like them to sign on with me. Two, I had to spend 20 minutes every day educating myself in fitness, also 20 minutes every day educating myself in sales, and 20 minutes each day educating myself on running a business. It didn't matter if I learned something from Facebook, a blog, a book, or a newspaper. I absorbed whatever I could from wherever I could. It was paramount that I stay sharp and focused on my goals. No excuses!

Now, if you think this might have been somewhat daunting when you consider everything I was doing, working, college, keeping my family together, small crying baby that wakes me up all night long, and doing training on the side, you are right! But I will tell you right now that you are going to go nowhere unless you are willing to sacrifice and put in the hard work and huge effort it will take you to get there. I wanted to succeed at something more. It is the reason I uprooted my family and came to America. It would be a great disservice and insult to them for me to do less. This is what kept me going. So, there I was with all these goals to complete on top of all my other responsibilities and let me tell you that I barely reached them. I was so far outside of my comfort zone here. Way out! I knew what I wanted to do. I had just never thought about something this big before!

But I kept on writing. This time I wrote down the principles of starting a business and what I needed to do to make it happen. I thought okay, let's write down everything I will need to do to actually open up a business, and I set the goals. Here's the thing. In the big box gym where I worked, everything was set by the management of the company. The guidelines and rules were laid out, and you followed them. It was simple. I wanted to get out of this comfort zone, and see if I could manage my own business, be my own management. I thought, if I could keep myself accountable to my goals, I could do it! I started out with ten things I knew I would have to accomplish daily. On top of that there were ten to fifteen other things I needed to accomplish to get the business going. For example, I knew I needed to get licensed to run a business and to do that, I needed an LLC. I also needed an EIN number for the IRS. I needed to talk to an accountant to find out what I needed to do and then acquire an accounting software program that I could master. I needed a real estate agent to find me space. Then there was the line of credit I needed to secure from the bank to be able to have some financial leverage. And on and on…

When you have a vision, it can seem overwhelming. But when you start to write it down, and you begin to define the steps to get you there, things begin to take shape and look doable. I am not talking about big deals here. The steps will be small at first. But with the completion of each one you have set for yourself, you will make another stride in the right direction. And with each stride, you will feel this what I call, do-ability, rise up. It is very freeing. Because now you can easily see and quantify the progress you are making toward reaching your vision. Every time you cross something off your list you automatically level up to the next challenge. Each time you reach that next goal your confidence builds, and this is where you gain momentum. Keeping the momentum going is what serves you. It's the fuel that gets you to the next level and the next and the next...

Look, I don't have a formula for setting my goals. I think we all do things a little differently. It is up to each of us individually to work in our own way. When I write out on paper the things that I want, I begin to see the path. For me, I make columns on the paper that have headings. Under each heading, I write down my thoughts, and as my thoughts spell out on the paper, the goals automatically appear. Then I write down all the things I need to do to accomplish my goals. You know, I keep legal pads everywhere in my studio where I train my clients. I have notes next to my phone and next to my bed. Notepads are everywhere. I am constantly writing and writing and writing. Every thought that gets me excited gets written down! Otherwise, I will forget it. As things flow out of me, they give me perspective and a reality check that I know I can't get any other way. You may do this differently, and that is okay. What I do know is that your goals need to be doable and keep fueling the momentum. Stay totally aware and write, write, write! Let your goals give you the momentum that keeps propelling you forward and leveling up!

I never took out a loan for my business. At the time I was putting all of this together, I believed that as long as I was making it with crappy equipment, I actually had a chance. It's not that I am cheap, I just didn't have money for the high-end stuff. Five years was exactly how long it took me to get up enough guts and equipment to leave my secure job and stand on my own! That being said, I will be forever thankful to my former boss, the management, my co-trainers, and all the people from that gym. I've made so many great memories, learned a lot, and made great friendships while working there. That gym gave me the start I needed to create my little empire. In the meantime, I took that equipment, and I worked long and hard, starting my business with it. You might say if I could do that with the rusty equipment I was using, I was destined for the success I have today. But not without the effort and hard work I put in to get me here.

So, start small with your goals. Write down two small tasks that you need to complete. Each time you complete one, cross it off. Then write down two more. Each time you do this, things will seem more and more doable. Sometimes the goals seem like they might be long-term, but then they become a simple two-day goal. You don't know until you set them down on paper. What I can tell you is that you will suddenly find yourself with a list of 30 things you need to do. And yes, some might be daily and some long-term. But every time you cross one off of your list, you level up, and you will have gained so much mental strength along the way. You might think of it like playing a video game if you are a gamer. In a video game, when you level up, you can get a new weapon. If you level up again, you might get a new super-power. The idea is that each time you keep moving up a level, the goal gets closer, and as you level up, you gain more tools to make things happen. That's a confidence builder for sure. That's what I call momentum!

"The greater danger for most of us isn't that our aim is too high and miss it, but that it is too low and we reach it."

Michelangelo

BO'S HOMEWORK

Write down a simple goal.

_____

_____

_____

_____

Create two small tasks to do that will help you to complete the goal.

_____

_____

_____

_____

When you have completed them, cross them off.

Write down a new goal and so on...

Chapter Three

Stay Sore

One thing I will never do to my clients is to tell them to do something or preach to them about something that I haven't tried first. There is not a mental or physical exercise that I have not tried and improved myself before I teach it to others. I am honest and transparent with all of my clients, and they respect me for it. I always tell my clients to "Stay Sore." It means staying humbled by the heavyweight of life and learning to lift it up so you can become stronger, seek out the discomfort/pain, which will make you stronger. I follow this myself, and my clients know and understand it.

The phrase "Stay Sore" means a lot to me! This is how I understand life. This is how life works. You can't avoid it. You have no choice but to live by this principle. Nothing good comes easy. If you want something good, you need to put work in. This is why I love the health and fitness industry so much. Here you cannot cheat the system. You get out exactly what you put in. It doesn't matter if it's health or fitness! If you want certain results, you need to do certain things, and you'll get there for sure. There is no other way. If I would only have a penny for every time a client told me they have tried everything and still don't see any results.

Most people that come to me asking for advice usually tune out if I start saying things potentially uncomfortable for them to hear. They only want me to say what they want to hear. But that's almost never the case. And then they come back a few months later and ask again in the hope that my answer has changed. Some people have done this for many years now. I'm not judging anyone, I am just trying to say that it is hard to change. It is much easier to keep looking around for a shortcut, again and again. It is hard to do something you don't feel like doing. It is hard to stop eating things that make you feel good (temporarily). It is hard to skip dessert or alcohol when family and friends gather around the table and put pressure on you without any regard for your health. It is hard to enjoy the amazing taste of fresh fruit and vegetables when all your taste buds have known for the past 10-15 years is tasting the opposite like sweet-and-sour chicken, caramel with salt on it, salty pizza with pineapple and other less healthy stuff. Of course, your taste buds won't like raw vegetables after that. Ok, I'm getting off-topic here... Yes, it is hard to change your habits. I totally understand this. But then again, if you want something, you have to work for it. I understand that this chapter may sound very discouraging and uncomfortable for many, but please don't give up. Keep reading, there might be some light and encouragement at the end of this chapter.

The gym teaches you that you have to get way out of your comfort zone (workout and nutrition) in order to achieve the health and looks you want, and you cannot cheat or shortcut this process. But when you think about it, this exact same lesson applies to every single aspect of life. If you want a good education, you need to study hard for years. Sometimes day and night in order to pass your exams. Sometimes you'll have great teachers, and sometimes you'll have not such great teachers, and you'll have to work even harder than you originally thought, only to get a decent grade. If you want a promotion or raise at work, you'll need to outwork your coworkers. If you want a better house or car you will need to make more money, which usually means you will need to work more. If you want to work smarter instead of harder you will need to put a lot of effort into learning to do so. If you want to play an instrument good enough for people to actually enjoy it, not just give you a fake smile so they don't hurt your feelings, you have to put in endless hours of practice. If you want to have a family you will have to work on your relationship. Yes, you need to work on your relationship if you want it to last and grow. You will have to go through the pain of labor if you want to see the smile of your child. If you don't like the way you feel you have to work on changing your lifestyle and habits. If you don't like having anxiety and/or depression you will have to take uncomfortable action as well in order to improve your mental or emotional state. It won't go away by itself. I hope you see where I am going with this. The hardest kind of work is working on yourself.

Everything that is worth something requires challenging and uncomfortable action at first. The key is "at first." Most people are so terrified of making that first uncomfortable step that they never even give themselves a chance to see if it's really that bad. About 9 out of 10 clients that I have trained in the past decade secretly love working out. They are afraid to admit it because I will say, "told you so." At first, most people have a super hard time coming into my gym. They don't want to be pushed on the workout floor. They don't want to be judged by others. They don't want to be judged by the fitness trainer. They don't want to be sweaty, out of breath, and sore after the workout. But give them a few weeks of training, and they become best friends with the trainer. Also that workout usually becomes the best part of their day. That's just how it works. And this is one of the biggest lessons I want you to get out of this book: being sore, getting out of your comfort zone and being challenged is not always necessarily as bad as you paint it in your head. Give it a chance and maybe, just maybe, you'll fall in love with that challenge that makes you better.

There are 3 truths to the concept of "Stay Sore," which I want you to understand. And please apply this to all aspects of your life, not just the gym.

1. Maintenance takes work. If you stop working out, your muscles, heart, and lung capacity will atrophy. Which means decline always comes by default.

2. Growth and improvement require new levels of discomfort. Otherwise, your body has no reason to change.

3. If you start feeling comfortable, see truth #1

"Nothing good comes easy."

Bo Skitsko

BO'S HOMEWORK

Have you ever achieved something truly great without putting work into it?

_____

_____

_____

_____

After you finally have achieved something truly great, how many times did you regret putting in that hard work?

_____

_____

_____

_____

Chapter Four

Action

Most of the big gurus and all the books that I read say that you have to set your mind on a path, and then your body will follow. I agree with that 100%. If your mind is strong and you work on your physical strength, your body will get there. It's like doing a heavy squat. If you do decide to do a squat, your body will figure out how to bend your knees and back to somehow do it, even if your form isn't the best. But if your mindset isn't there, maybe you had a bad day or are going through personal stuff, and you aren't in the game, nothing's going to work for you. Just stepping back and waiting for your mind to clear isn't going to do much either. You need to take action! This is key! I like Tony Robbins for his take on this. He talks about the idea that when you're depressed and life feels heavy on your shoulders, you need to straighten yourself up and stand up tall. Put your shoulders back and chest up, hold your chin up high, and things will just automatically look better. When you are standing tall and proud, it's hard to be depressed. You just feel differently about yourself, like you can conquer things! This inspires action, and that brings momentum back into play.

Here's another example. Take your appetite. Say you're not hungry, but you see everyone sitting down to eat or even a commercial about food on TV and suddenly, just from watching this ad, you have acquired an appetite. This happens in your body before you've even processed it in your mind. The same can happen when you're working out. I have clients that have told me they've driven by my studio several days in a week for the past 3, 4, or 6 months thinking they should go in Someday. Because of this, "Someday" has become my very favorite day of the week. The story usually goes like this, "I'll go in on Sunday, Monday, Tuesday, Wednesday, Thursday…or Someday!" So, it took them a long time to contemplate taking action to do something good for themselves. Then at some point, they realized that they just needed to step up and go inside.

Here's the thing. You need to have the right mindset, true. But there are times when you need to let your body lead your mind. Here's why. Our body instinctively knows what it needs. The problem with our minds is that they often have to catch up to that idea. Our minds like to play these little tricks on us that ultimately hold us back. For instance, your mind will fill you with all the excuses it can come up with to keep you from doing the right thing. We humans are very good at sabotaging ourselves in this way. This is how I explain it to my clients. The human body, whether you believe in evolution or creation, by its nature, is designed to protect you.

For example, if you spend a lot of time in the sun, your skin will darken or tan. This is your body's way of protecting you from burning. When you chop wood, you build up callouses on your hands. This is also your body's way of thickening your skin to protect it from tearing. When you start working out at the gym, things are going to suck at first. You know this in your mind. That's when your mind starts playing its little games by telling you it's going to be hard, and it's going to hurt. But once you start working out and your body begins to feel the amazing changes happening and that you are serious, it's going to work to protect you; but in a different way. By putting stress on your muscles, on your tendons and ligaments, on your bones, on your joints, even on your lungs, heart and other organs, your body will have to make all these things stronger and more efficient in order to make that sensation less stressful next time you work out (Wolff's law). Next time you are in the gym, you take this new strength and workout even harder so your body has to adapt to the new stimulus and become even better. This is what fitness is all about in a nutshell – you take uncomfortable action, and your body adapts to make it less uncomfortable, to protect you. In sports science theory, this is called super-compensation. Your body knows that this protection is coming from the new strength you are building. Now is when your mindset will begin to change into positive re-enforcement of your workouts and allow your body to keep strengthening. You might even get to where you look forward to your workouts because, at this point, you have already experienced the amazing benefits. What I can, and do, guarantee my clients is that their mindset will shift from a negative mentality to a positive mentality that wants to keep growing and "protecting" their strength.

So, you made it to the gym even though you didn't want to go. You don't look forward to it, but you start moving and working out and listening to the instructor. You see other people sweating, struggling, but enjoying themselves. You start sweating, huffing and puffing. Your adrenaline, your serotonin, and dopamine levels start to go up in response to the exercise. Weirdly enough, instead of regretting making this decision to step into the gym, you start feeling proud and accomplished. Your sore and burning muscles start to make you feel alive for the first time in a long time.

The point to all of this is that making the right decision is not always as easy and simple as it should be. Deep down, we usually know what the right decision is. And yes, if you make a decision, your body will follow your mind. But the problem is that we live in a society where our decision-making abilities are broken. Our minds seem to be corrupted by our phone, by unrealistic Instagram pictures, by the negative news on TV, by endless homework from school/college, by working overtime, by doctor appointments, by medication, by other people's opinions and expectations. I could keep going on and on. Every other person I work with has some sort of anxiety or depression. I think it's safe to say that 9 out of 10 people that come to train in my studio feel overwhelmed by life. The stressful and hectic lifestyle, information overload, and the speed at which society lives right now make it almost impossible to use our brains to make correct, strong, and firm decisions. If your mind is broken, then let your body just take action. I trust you to know what the right action is. We all know what the right action is. If you want to lose weight, then eat less and workout more. If you want a better job then go and apply, don't procrastinate. If you want to have a better education then take the first class. If you want better health then take ownership of your habits. If you want a better family or relationship then turn off your phone and hold your wife's or husband's hand. If you can't make yourself decide something, then take the first step, and your mind will fall in love with the outcome and reward you.

"Inaction breeds doubt and fear. Action breeds confidence and courage. If you want to conquer fear, do not sit home and think about it. Go out and get busy."

Dale Carnegie

BO'S HOMEWORK

Do you have any goals right now where you are afraid to take the first step towards them? Write them down.

_____

_____

_____

_____

Write down why you are afraid to take the first step.

_____

_____

_____

_____

Chapter Five

Nothing Good Comes Easy

I hate the term "selling." I really do. I don't even refer to it like that because I am all about "service." Serving is what I believe I am here to do. I am here to serve my clients so they can lead better lives.

Now, I like to think that I can talk to anybody these days. Some might say that I am an extrovert. I can feel comfortable with a group or an individual, and I enjoy talking with people. I don't take this for granted, mind you. Getting here, to this point, has not been easy. Naturally, I am pretty quiet and shy. Speaking to a group of people or even to just one new person used to paralyze me. That was one of the scariest things I had to overcome. I knew that I had to attack this fear and discomfort if I wanted to be able to help people for a living. Anything worth doing is never going to be easy. I just somehow knew when I began this journey that I was going to have to get out of my own skin and go after the things I wanted and believed in. That included offering my services to people I didn't know so that they could benefit from my training. For sure, no one was going to do it for me. It was going to be totally on me to make things happen, just like it is on you to make things happen for you.

When I first started at the big box gym working as a trainer, the manager would always hand me scripted texts that I had to learn and say to potential customers. It was the most uncomfortable feeling. I really couldn't get into it because it was too stiff and formulated. It was extremely uncomfortable for me to parrot this information to potential clients and expect them to buy into it. I think it was demeaning to them too. I could sense that the people didn't like it. They could feel my stiffness and the pressure we were putting on them to sign on. It made everyone uncomfortable, and I never picked up one client using that formula. There was no emotion in it. I sounded like a robot just trying to extract money from them. And, as I said, I got no takers. That's when I figured out that something had to change in how I was doing things. That was when I realized the way to making this work was to have a better understanding of what I wanted to do. And I realized that the thing I truly wanted to do was to serve the people, not sell to people.

So, I set about reformulating the way I was communicating with people. I changed from selling to serving. I admit that I used the script they had given me to help outline what and how I wanted to communicate. But I was using them as tools now rather than a scripted speech. I began engaging with people and getting to know them. I found that I wanted, not needed, to find out about them as a person. I wanted to know everything. I wanted to understand their goals. I wanted to know why they wanted to start now, what motivated them, what they thought would be the result of their efforts. I even asked about family and kids. I wanted to know them inside and out. I realized that this is where I could reach them at their core. I would also share some of my story with them, and that created empathy between us. For me, this is what it is about. Because I am here to help you and my clients lead better and stronger lives. That includes the inside as much as the outside. This was not something that happened overnight, however. The first time I tried it, I was incredibly bad. I am certain the person thought I was a bumbling fool and wasn't really sure about signing up with me. And, at first, I really tried to forget about that experience as soon as I was done. But I didn't let myself forget. And this is a very important lesson. You cannot let yourself forget uncomfortable or bad situations.

They are your test. They are your perfect classroom for learning. So, this was my test. I knew that I had to learn from it so that I could improve and keep on improving with each step. These experiences took me way outside of my comfort zone once again. I knew that each time I made my pitch, I would get better at it. But that didn't stop the terror I felt when I tried it those first few times with my broken accent. I kept at it, though, because I knew it would take practice. And there is no other way to help people with my knowledge other than having them sign up with me.

I will be honest and tell you that the first time you step out, it is going to be rough. The second time you might be a little bit better at it. By the third time, your brain will start to get excited, and then you'll notice things starting to take shape. Your mindset will begin to shift over to a different way of looking at things. And as you keep on going, I guarantee that you will get more comfortable and better and better until you finally find your stride. The key is to not give up because it's hard. It's going to be hard! You don't build more muscle if you lift the same weight all the time, right? You need to level up and keep increasing the weight to build more muscle. You don't learn new things by reading the same book over and over. You don't get paid more by doing the same work the same way. It's the same with exercising your sales techniques. Each time you present your service to a potential client, you need to up your game. In this way, you will continue to grow and get better. If you make a mistake or feel that you did not do well, look at it, touch it, feel it. Figure out why and use that information to improve next time. These days I don't even sell anymore; I just help people.

I'm far from being old yet. But I have learned a lot in my short time here on earth. When I first came to America, all I wanted to do was survive. That is how I ended up cleaning toilets. I did not know any English, but I could do this without speaking to anyone. For most immigrants, there's only a handful of jobs you can do when you don't know the language. You can clean toilets or become a delivery driver or truck driver. You can get into construction or cleaning jobs. Things that don't require you speaking to people. But then I started realizing that I was hanging out with the same people, and my language wasn't getting any better. I wasn't learning anything because we were all still speaking our own language and doing the same thing day in and day out. It was comfortable. Well, comfortable wasn't getting me anywhere, right? I knew I had to change what I was doing and get out of that comfortable place.

So, one day, I decided that I would strive for better. I went out of my way to get out of my comfort zone and applied for a job at a fast-food place, delivering sandwiches. I actually had to talk to people there. My worst nightmare was taking orders on the phone. When you are in front of people, you can make hand gestures to get your point across. You can't do that on the phone. I had to listen very hard and then explain the orders back to them. And I would constantly screw up addresses for which I had to pay the person's check out of my own pocket because of the botched delivery. Then there was the credit card information I got wrong. The charges would be denied again and again. And the money to cover it would go out of my check. It's a wonder I even made a nickel. In fact, I'm not sure I made much money at that job at all after paying for all of my mistakes. It was very stressful! It was what you call "baptism by fire!" But I tell you this, after about 6 months of doing this...and thank God I kept my job that long...after about 6 months, I was speaking English pretty well.

So, when I talk about discomfort, I am telling you that you need to keep running toward the pain and accept it. Acknowledge that you're going to go through some crazy hard stuff and get ready to feel it! Pain can be good. It happens in two ways. Physical pain tells your body what you can and/or should not do. If your knees or back hurt while you are doing squats, it is because your form is bad. This is the kind of pain that makes you notice and pay attention to your body so you can protect it. It tells you when something is wrong and to protect yourself.

Mental pain, on the other hand, can be used as fuel to keep your momentum going. It helps you to adjust. In my own example, it was painful to take orders on the phone for the sandwich shop because I had no clue what the people were talking about. But I took that pain and used it to adjust my way of thinking. I started to learn English that I so desperately needed to keep growing.

Pain, whether physical or mental, guides us and keeps us moving in the right direction on our path. So, don't shy away from it. It is part of building your confidence. You can apply this to every part of life. Whether it's a personal relationship or business sales and marketing strategies or working with new people, you will start to elevate yourself by putting in the hard work. I have empathy for you because I know what it is like. I know that taking this uncomfortable and painful step will be the catalyst for going out and grabbing the better life you seek. I tell you now that you will become stronger at all that you do, and that strength will allow you to accomplish amazing things. And I will be very excited about the strides you will make as you move out of your comfort zone and start to take steps toward a better life for yourself.

Nothing that is worth doing or living is going to come easy. If it does, you won't have any appreciation for it, and that is destructive. If you want to grow, you have to allow yourself to get uncomfortable. Learn from your discomfort. It takes getting outside your head and comfort place to gain the courage and confidence to keep moving forward. This is nothing new to you I am sure. We have all learned about it somewhere and somehow. If you stay in your comfort zone all the time, you will not grow and move forward. Why? Because you will never allow yourself to experience anything outside of your current state of being. If you don't experience anything new, how will you learn anything?

"I am a great believer in luck, and I find the harder I work, the more I have of it."

Thomas Jefferson

BO'S HOMEWORK

Think of something that you feel uncomfortable doing yet want the result of it.

What is the worst thing that could happen if you do it?

_____

_____

_____

_____

What if you never actually go after what you desire so much? How does this thought make you feel?

_____

_____

_____

_____

Chapter Six

No Time for Anxiety

When my clients come to me, I am often nervous. It is a responsibility that I take very seriously. Meaning, I realize that they are coming to me because I am the expert and their mentor. So, I cannot afford to show them my nerves or any weakness. I must be confident and make them feel that I know exactly what I am here for and how to guide them, right? Because they are here for one purpose, and that is to work with me. They are seeking someone stronger to guide them. When my client shows up, I flip my switch! I show myself as the most confident person you know. I know exactly what to say and let them know that I am totally and completely here for them. Now they have the confidence in knowing that I've got this, and more importantly, we've got this together!

Later on, when everyone is gone, and I am alone, I collapse, and my switch flips off again. This is when I am vulnerable to all of the anxieties that plague me every day. I end up not sleeping until 4:00 a.m. because I am overtaken by my own personal terrors. I worry about the business and how it is doing because this is how I am taking care of my family. I worry about my clients and if their workouts went well. If the things we have talked about and the things I have taught them are going to help them in more than just the fitness aspect of life. After a whole day of helping other people, listening to their problems inside and outside of the gym, truly caring for them, putting them first, and serving them, I burn out. When the last person leaves the studio, I close the door, collapse on my office chair and quietly say to myself: "Wow, another day. You made it. You helped them." I worry about signing on new clients to grow or at least sustain the business. Will there be enough clients for me to be able to pay my bills? I worry about my kids and how they are doing. I essentially become this humbled and overthinking boy who is anxious about everything in his life, from his business to his family. This is how every single day of my life looked when I first started.

When I let my overthinker take over, I would often get stuck in my own pool of fear and anxiety. It would just drag me down! My heart would be beating fast, and I was sweating. I couldn't sleep because I was up for hours worrying.

Sometimes my stomach hurt so bad and my back ached because I was so tensed up. If I didn't have too much to worry about, I could create more. That is the nature of the overthinker. This overwhelming anxiety would just feed off of itself, it seemed. And it was affecting me mentally and physically.

I understand that this might sound silly or dramatic. But consider the fact that I was a young immigrant without any connections or knowledge of the business. And in the beginning everything in the business was on my shoulders: programing, cleaning, repairing, marketing, selling, posting on social media every day, building a website, permits, licenses, outside and inside signage, customer support, gym management software, credit card processing, accounting, taxes, event planning, email automation and newsletters, business phone line, copywriting for targeted and organic ads, video editing, following up with clients, tons of spreadsheets, networking, expos and so much more. All the while, I still had to train people about 8-10 hours a day. Also, don't forget, my income was the only income for our household. All that can give you some anxiety.

Then I heard about a guy, Bedros Keuilian. He is the founder of the franchise Fit Body Boot Camp. He came from humble beginnings as a personal trainer, just like me. What he did, though, was to become so good at it that he was able to turn it into a million-dollar business through a series of savvy decisions. He realized that people like me who do personal training need mentoring of our own so that we can establish and build our business effectively. We need to gain the necessary marketing and sales skills to be able to acquire new clients and keep growing. The idea was really genius. And the lessons he teaches have helped me a lot.

So, I bought and read his book, "Man Up! How to Cut the Bullshit and Kick @ss in Business and Life". It's a great book that I am happy to recommend here. The over-riding message that resonated from this book for me was that the more action you take, the less time you will have for anxiety. Think about this for a minute, and it will make total sense. When you are taking action, your brain stays focused on the task at hand. There is no space in your brain for your overthinker to take over and fill you with dread. The less time you have to spend with your overthinker, the better! Putting yourself into action mode leaves no space for the anxiety to creep in. I believe this is one of the best lessons I have ever learned. And I share it with you here because it will be one of the best lessons I believe you will learn. It is that big!

I realized that I spend way more time worrying about the things that I need to do than actually getting them done. The second I started taking real action, not only did my business grow, but also my anxiety had no chance to take over and cause me to worry unnecessarily about things. By the time I had a second to worry about the tasks that need to be done, they were already taken care of. When I found myself with so much on my mind that I wasn't able to sleep at night, I made a decision. Instead of feeling sorry for myself and wasting time watching YouTube videos on my phone all night, I decided that I would become a published author. That's when I started working on this book, which by now is a much different book than when I first started playing around with ideas for it.

I am going to share something with you for the first time in this book. Here is how I look at overthinking. When you are driving down the highway at 65 mph, and someone cuts you off, you don't have time to think. Everything you do is a pure reflex. Your body kicks into gear, reacts, and boom, you're out of the way. Nine and a half times out of ten when this happens, you're okay. You might be pissed off at the other person, but you're fine, and you can keep on going. Whenever you need it, your body knows what to do. It creates an instant and spontaneous reaction to what is going on. Since you are already driving fast, the body just reacts, and you keep going. It's like the faster you are going, the easier it is for you to make a decision or correction without too much thought put into it. Let's say we turn this around, and you're riding along in a neighborhood at about 30 mph. There is a stoplight ahead. As you are approaching the stoplight, the light is turning from green to yellow. You have to make a decision. Should you hit the brakes and stop, or do you have enough time to still blow through? You think about it all the way to the light. Some will stop, but some will blow through. It's here when you have a lot of time to think about what to do that you tend to make the wrong decision; you're overthinking it. It's a simplistic way to look at it, but it gets the point across.

This is exactly what happens when that overthinker kicks your anxieties into overdrive! When you have too much time to think, it's easier to over analyze everything and end up on the wrong path. So, the faster you go, the easier it is to just let things unfold and happen. You won't have the time to overthink them and hesitate! Hesitation is what tends to mess us up.

It's all about how hesitation makes all your worst fears come true. If you give yourself too many options and you're trying to analyze every detail so that everything comes out perfectly, that is when you create the most worry. And the more worrying you do, the more options you create, the harder the decision becomes. At the end of the day, you end up talking yourself into and out of so many options that your focus starts to fade. The lesson I give you here is to stick with your gut feeling! Ninety times out of one hundred, it is usually the right one. Don't let yourself get overwhelmed with too many choices and options. You'll only end up talking yourself out of what you knew was the right thing to do from the start! The goal is to create action in your life. The more action, the less time you will have to overthink things. And the more you put on the line, the more you will accomplish. The more productive you are, the easier it is to keep the ball bouncing, and the less time you'll have to talk yourself out of things. So, the way I look at it is that the more productive activity going on, the more you condense time. You hit one goal and then another and another. The list of things that need to get done keeps getting checked off, and you're not thinking too much about it; you're just doing it. It keeps the negative thoughts out and the positive momentum pushing forward.

Ah, then, here's the kicker! And it's beautiful. If you make the wrong decision, you're not really stuck with it. In most cases, you can pivot and still make it right again, later on down the road. I'm not talking about the kinds of decisions that are hurtful and last for life. I'm talking about regular business stuff, work, house, car... There is no doubt in business that you're going to lose out once in a while. It's the nature of the beast. So, maybe you lose on a bad decision. That's okay. You can still pivot, learn from it, and make it right.

To sum it all up, when there is no action, you will overthink things. When there is action all around you, you don't have time to worry about it because you are constantly in a state of movement. Your focus and attention are directed toward completing the tasks at hand. Every completed task makes you feel accomplished, proud, and even happy. Try to feel anxiety or any negative thoughts when you are accomplished, proud, and happy!

"Nothing diminishes anxiety faster than action."

Walter Anderson

BO'S HOMEWORK

What's keeping you up at night?

_____

_____

_____

_____

Do you feel like a victim when anxiety kicks in?

_____

_____

_____

_____

What actions could you be taking right now that would help move these things forward and get them out of your head?

_____

_____

_____

_____

Chapter Seven

When You Invest, You Commit

Hey, I'm a procrastinator at heart. I work best under the kind of pressure that comes with waiting until the last minute. I'm what some would call the "photo finish" guy. I learned this about myself early on. If you're going to give me two weeks to do something, I'm going to be at the doorstep of the deadline hammering away to get it done on time. If you give me a year, it's going to be a year. That is really who I am. I don't advise it for my clients or anyone else. My strength lies in knowing who I am. By knowing my strengths and weaknesses, I can actually do something about it. What I do well, though, is to continue to create momentum. I've said this previously in the book …it's the momentum that carries me through to the end.

If I can get the momentum going and keep it going, then I'm good. Create action and momentum, and you'll get past the anxiety and overthinking. You'll be moving faster and as we know, the faster you go, the more effective and easier the decisions come. We all need a spark. So, do whatever you have to do to ignite the fire in you to create your own momentum. Read books, go to seminars, meditate, or work out. You can make it a daily, weekly, or monthly goal or practice.

I use external factors to motivate me and light the spark when my inner motivation decides to be a brat that day. Then I can keep going and find that inner fire and get the ball rolling. That's where I find my inner motivation. I schedule my clients as early as I can. That way, I have to get up and get moving. If I were to schedule them for noon, I wouldn't even roll out of bed until after 11:00 a.m. So, I start my clients off at 5:30 a.m. That way, I have to get up and moving early. I like starting early. This forces me to be productive, focused, and accomplished before most people even start their day. It's a discomfort that I use to motivate myself. Because as I said earlier, I run toward discomfort in order to grow. If I can help to change a person's fitness and life early in the morning, then the rest of the day, I'm Superman!

So, lots of people aren't trainers or coaches. That's why they need me. What I do for them is hold them accountable. When you hire me, you are motivating yourself to do what you need to do because you know that I will keep you accountable for meeting your goals. Look, even the best athletes in the world, Olympic athletes, bodybuilders, sprinters, swimmers, skaters, etc., who know what they need have trainers and coaches. Why? Because it is the trainers and coaches that hold them accountable and keep them on track. Every single one of them knows what to do, but they still need a coach.

If a world-class athlete knows he needs a coach to keep him accountable, so should you and I. The coach or mentor is the one that will prevent us from overthinking and making the poor decision. Look, in a way, my clients are the ones that keep me accountable because I have a responsibility to them. It all works together. There are no short cuts in life. But if you hire someone who has already been there, that can teach you from the mistakes they've already made, you're going to be way ahead of the game. No amount of money is going to be too much to get that valuable kind of training and/or knowledge. It is crucial to cutting your long path to success in half. I did it myself. I didn't have any money at the time, but I still hired Tim Lyons from ProFit Marketing Solutions to help me out. I know how to train my clients and how to give them results. But in the beginning, I had no idea how to package it into a real business. Just as my clients hire me as a professional to help them with their health and fitness, the exact same way, I hired Tim Lyons as a mentor to teach me about business. I did not think of it as an expense but as an investment. It was one of the best investments I ever made in myself. Most of the lessons he taught me I kind of already knew. What he did was to help me put together a structured plan that held me accountable. He set up guidelines and deadlines for me to meet. I had to show up and actually do all the things I had been procrastinating on because I had invested thousands of dollars that I couldn't even afford. However, I couldn't afford not to invest in myself. I knew most of these lessons from books, videos, seminars, and even common sense. But the second I put value on it, my business and I started growing.

I had a few plans for my business already when I hired Tim as my mentor and coach. I had it in my mind that my business would be at a certain level within 3 to 4 years. After I was done with Tim, at only eight weeks into it, I had my plan outlined and structured with measurable goals and deadlines all set up. I was ready to go.

The only short cut worth taking on your path to creating your own success is to invest in a coach or mentor that has already been there. Sit down, shut up, and listen to the lessons they are teaching you. It will save you unbelievable time and aggravation if you are willing to learn from the experiences they share, whether successes or mistakes. Don't question what they tell you until you've heard and absorbed it all. Review and analyze the things they are willing to share with you. You can learn so much when you stop talking and listen to them. In the end, you are even allowed to disagree. But just remember this: it is very hard to learn something by talking, therefore listen first and only then speak.

I am a firm believer that where you put your money is where you will give your most attention. When you invest in something with your hard-earned money, you have now placed value on it. That makes you stand up and pay attention. Why would you invest your money and then not try to reap the benefits? Put down your money, and you will generally work hard to profit from that investment. What I have learned from being in business is that if you aren't willing to value it and invest back into it, it really doesn't have any value.

Here's a good example of what I'm talking about. I used to run ads on Facebook for my fitness studio that would advertise, "First workout FREE!". People would schedule and then never show up. Can you believe it? They would actually sign up for it and then blow it off. I could not wrap my head around it. I mean, what did they have to lose by coming to a free session? I really thought people would like this and take advantage of it. Boy, was I surprised…and wrong! No one showed up. And I would be left sitting there pissed off because they blew me off.

What I know now is that there is no value in "free"! There I was, sitting there, wasting my time because I had placed no value on my own work. And because I had placed no value on it, neither did the people that signed up for it. Something for free has literally no value to people. So, I took that away and learned from it. I started charging people for the first consultation. I placed a monetary value on it so that they felt they had to show up because they had paid for it. Well, BOOM! People that signed up then would show up! Why, because it now had value to them. The bottom line is that if you pay for something, you value it. It's not like I just wanted their money. I wanted their attention. But their attention was going to be where their money was. "At the end of the day, you are the one that creates the need for me to charge you."

If people don't pay for your service, they aren't going to care what you say to them or what you try to teach them. The more value you place on something, the more worth it has to people. This is very true. For instance, it is September right now, and I have already read 31 new books on business this year. Well, half of them I listen to while I am working out. The others I read in my leisure time if you can even call it that. Anyway, these books cost about $15.00 each on average. You can read them and get some things out of them if you are paying good attention. But what if you pay ten-grand for a month of training? Well, all of a sudden, the value of the information you are getting goes way, way up! It could even be the same lessons and information you got out of the books, but because you spent a lot more money on the training, those lessons and words are worth incredibly more to you. This would suggest that there is some magic created by paying for something, right?

Whatever it is that you want to improve or grow in your life, it will never reach peak potential unless you put crazy and sometimes even risky amounts of value on it.

"Don't tell me where your priorities are. Show me where you spend your money, and I'll tell you what they are."

James W. Frick

BO'S HOMEWORK

How much of an investment are you willing to make in yourself?

_____

_____

_____

_____

Chapter Eight

Remove the Safety Net

I'm going to talk here about removing your safety net and opening yourself up to failure. That's a scary thought, right? Here you are trying to make life-changing decisions and go after the things you want in life, and now I'm telling you that if you're going to succeed, you have to give up your fall back, your security in case things don't work out. The fact is, there is a high probability you will fail at something. But I believe that the safety nets hold us back. That's often the truth. Because when you remove the safety net, you have no choice but to take the necessary actions and force yourself to succeed.

Right? So, the best thing you can do is to fail. This is how you will learn what not to do, or perhaps what to do. It's the path to growth! However, if you're going to fail, and you will, you need to fail quickly and early on when the potential for damage is minimal. I cannot stress this enough. Starting out, my business was very small. In that first year, I only made about $20k working my behind off. That's not a lot, but it's also not a lot to lose. I knew that I wanted to be doing more, but I also had to weigh the risk of how much I could do and potentially lose. Rather than going big out of the gate, I started small. To help it grow, but with minimal financial risk, if it failed, I tried a lot of different things. I tried to create 16 different prototypes of t-shirts and offer them to my clients to see which would work and which not. I tried different variations of a boot camp class. I even tried yoga classes. In the first year every time they saw me, my clients figured I was going to have something new for them to try. I bought and sold lots of different workout equipment to see what works and what fails. It was a calculated effort on my part to try to increase my income so that I could save my money and not put the whole business at risk later on when it gets bigger. I made sure that none of those small investments, if they failed, were going to be significant enough to have a negative impact on my ability to support my family.

This is the key thing to think about. I have talked about failing and removing safety nets in order to grow. You also need to be very careful and diligent about how you are going to proceed when you do make decisions to do something bigger. For instance, right now, I am in the process of planning a move to a bigger facility. But before I do that, I will be trying things out so that I start with a clean sheet with proven or unproven plans and services. Instead of jumping right into it, I am staying in my small facility for now so that I can try out different things and fail as much as I can before making the leap. As I have said, if I experience small failures here, they will have less of an impact than if I were to just jump right on getting into the larger facility. A failure at the level I am talking about requires a larger investment. The risk is higher, and if I lost the amount I need to invest in this project, it could really hurt! So, for now, I will continue to test things in my smaller environment before making this leap. When I am comfortable that I have the right things in place and the probability of success is fairly high, I will make my decision to move forward.

Most people would rather start a business when they are single because they don't have much to lose and nothing to worry about. That wouldn't work for me for two reasons. The obvious one was that I already had a wife and kids. The other having my wife and my kids were my motivation. If I was single, I would not have been so motivated. And I would probably have failed. Because of them, failure was never an option. Starting a business while your family is relying on your income is the definition of "removing your safety net." If the business I chose at that time wasn't going to work out when I was single, I would have found something else after a while. But now, I have a deep responsibility, and I will figure out how to make it work. There is no safety net. I will never work for me as hard as I work for the person next to me or even more so for my own family. This is what drives me. When my clients succeed, and I see how I have helped them to change their lives, it gives me more motivation to keep going than any amount of money or kudos. I will never have enough motivation for myself alone. It is other people's successes that keep me going.

What I want to get across here, though, is that you will fail. The important thing is that you need to control when and how that happens so that the damage is minimal, and the learning is greatest. Make sense? That's why I recommend failing quickly and early on before things are big.

Here's another example. I just printed shaker bottles for my clients with my gym's logo on it. Originally I wanted to create big insulated expensive water bottles. But then I thought if it fails, I'd rather fail quickly and painlessly. So I had plastic shaker bottles printed first to learn and see how my clients would react to them. This gave me more information about what my clients wanted and needed. This was a small investment in the scheme of things and not likely to bankrupt me. So, I ran with it.

There are much bigger things that can make or break you. How you finance your business, for instance. I never took out a loan for my business. I just knew that this would be a bad idea for me, and it would hurt big if it didn't work out. So many businesses fail, and then the owner is left with nothing or bankruptcy. You can lose everything you own if you make the wrong decision about your investment. There are people out there who have put up their home mortgages to finance their business only to have them fail and lose it all. You don't want to lose your home because your business didn't make it. You see what I'm getting at now? Failing quick, failing often, and especially failing early before making the big investments is how you stay in the game with minimal damage. Learn quietly but quickly while you are small, so you can explode when you are making big moves.

The biggest misconception I see getting into business is the thinking that you need money to make money. It really is a misconception! You can always find ways to market yourself and make money without investing a lot. Look at social media. It costs nothing, but you can advertise your services there and get clients. Today, you can even put up your own website without paying a lot of money to do it. It's very easy to set up a business these days. Twenty years ago, you would need to be a multi-million-dollar company to have a website. Today, anyone can set one up for very little. You can even get them for free if you don't mind ads on it. It's easier than ever! You just need some creativity, work ethic, and a passion for what you are doing. You don't need a lot of money to get going.

I mentioned before that I never took out a loan to start my business. This was a very calculated decision on my part. I did not want to have my family left holding a huge loan if something happened to me or the business failed. Again, my family is always my first consideration. So, I held on to old rusted equipment I had bought on Craigslist and used it for five years so that I could save up enough money to start my company. Also, I gave myself 5 years to learn everything I needed to be successful in the fitness industry. It took me longer than it should have for sure. But that was because I was hesitant to get going. And then there was the language barrier. Frankly, I was scared to open my business. I was scared to fail. Every night I would scroll through my phone and look for equipment. If I found something, I would hunt it down. I knew exactly how much it should cost and how much I had to spend and was willing to pay. I understood what a deal was. It was all about educating myself. This is why I can tell you that you can make it without much money in the beginning.

Nobody and nothing is perfect, right? There is no perfect person, perfect situation, perfect business. Nothing in this world is perfect, even the price of gold changes. What I say to my clients, especially in the beginning, is that you don't need to be perfect. Somewhere along the line, society decided that you had to be perfect in everything. Man, that is just not possible. No one starts out looking like a fitness model. You have to work to get there. So, I tell my clients that I don't need them to be perfect. I just need them to try the best that they can. This is enough! BUT…if I see they are not trying 100%, well then, I am going to kick their behinds! But you don't have to be perfect. Just do the best that you can. And that's what I did with my gym in the beginning. It was so far from perfect with all that rusty and not matching equipment. Turns out, my clients didn't sign up with me for a perfect gym, but because I was trying my absolute best to help them.

Building a business like this is a slow progression, but it is still progress. Staying stuck in one place is what keeps you down. Again, this goes back to taking action. If you stay in the same place all the time, you're never going to get anywhere. That's the truth. When you stay in the same place and never move, you begin to digress. I tell my clients that they need to keep moving. Otherwise, they are digressing. It's like having a savings account. In my opinion, the dumbest thing you can do is to have a savings account in a bank. That's because there is inflation and, if your money is just sitting there in that savings account, it's losing value. Why? Because of inflation. If you put $30k in the bank today, in twenty years, it's not going to be worth $30k. It will have lost value due to inflation. You have to keep it alive and increasing in value by investing it in a plan that grows.

There is no standing in place. When you just stand in place, nothing happens. There is no standing around or hanging out in the middle. I say, "Run in the direction of success!" If you can't run, then walk. If you can't walk, then crawl or lie down in the direction of where you want to be if that is what it takes. Nobody starts off at the pro level. No matter if you are a boxer, martial artist, business owner, or investor. Everyone has to work to get there!

When you listen to all the biggest sports celebrities out there, they will say that they are not competing with anyone else. They say that their biggest competition is themselves. They are constantly trying to level up from where they are. You set your own boundaries, and you can decrease or increase them as you choose. If you can expand them, you win. If you can't expand them, you lose. It doesn't matter who runs next to you. They may give you a little motivation to move faster because you will try to keep up and pass them. But at the end of the day, the winner will be the one who put in the effort to make himself better. Take Michael Jordan. What matters is the effort he puts in when he trains by himself, when nobody is watching him. Being on the court is his job, and his rock-solid performances out there are because he's continuously putting in time and effort going up against himself off the court.

It's all about doing the right thing and showing up when no one is watching that makes the difference. Setting the right expectations, and managing them whether it's meeting your financial goals, setting up your business or getting healthy. I still struggle with the idea of setting expectations because I believe that there is a fine line between setting expectations that are accomplishable and those that are crazy. For example, I'm sure some of you know Grant Cardone and his 10x rule. While I don't agree with everything that Cardone does and says, I do believe that the 10x rule is powerful. The one thing I have learned that works best for me is to set accomplishable goals. Say your business goal is to make $100k this year. If you achieve it, you're going to feel good about it. But what if you set a crazy goal to make $5M and you only make $200k? It's way off from your goal and seems like a big failure. But in reality, $200k is twice as much as $100k. Turns out failure comes in all kinds of different shapes, forms, and colors. If you are smart, you can even use failure to your advantage. Take for instance the gym. It is actually a good thing to fail in the gym. It means you pushed to your limits. By failing in the gym you create a reason for your body to become stronger and more fit.

So, here it is. You just have to want to do it. Don't sit around and dream or complain about it. Get it done! You don't need a lot of money to get started. Whatever it is you want to do, don't wait, don't be afraid. You just need to be creative and passionate about what you want to do. Don't wait to fail until you've invested a lot of time and money into your business. Start small and fail fast in the beginning when it will do the least harm. Success comes from learning from your mistakes and failures early on. Look around you at all the creative things you can do to get started with your dreams and see where they take you.

If you struggle with your health and fitness, then remove your safety net and expose yourself to an environment where there is no going back. For example, sign up for a whole year of training with a professional or some fitness classes. Now there are no more excuses, now you have to do the thing that will make you better. If you want to start a business, remove the safety net, and invest your money into it. Now you have no money, and you have to make it work. The beauty is that you can minimize the risk of failure by trying your trainer first, by trying your business as a side hustle first. But don't leave yourself a plan B or a comfortable safety net. Otherwise, you will be tempted to use it. Whatever your dream is, go after it hard and fast. The faster you go after your dreams, the smaller the bumps on your path will seem.

"Success is stumbling from failure to failure with no loss of enthusiasm."

Winston Churchill

BO'S HOMEWORK

Think of something you may have failed at.

What did you learn?

_____

_____

_____

_____

How do you apply the lesson going forward?

_____

_____

_____

_____

Chapter Nine

Every 1% Adds Up

Every single client that walks in my door, everyone, is looking for some big secret to unlock and poof... Let me tell you right now, there is NO SECRET! If someone tells you there is, they are full of bologna! If you really want a secret, it is in the small little decisions you make throughout the day, throughout the week and throughout the year that brings you closer to your goal. Every single decision you make in life will either get you closer to the goal or further away. If you want to be healthy, strong, and fit with a healthy mindset, watching that extra 20 minutes of TV at night isn't going to do a thing for you except take your eye off your goal. It would be far better for you to sleep for those 20 minutes. You will get better results the next day if you do. Your mind will be clearer, and you'll have much more energy to attack the next day. The

83

extra sleep clears the mind of clouds and gives you more thinking power for your business and family.

Every decision you make accumulates. One extra rep each day of a push-up or squat accumulates into a stronger body. One extra calorie can put you over the top, or one less calorie gets you closer to being leaner. It all adds up from each decision you make. One more rep, one more minute, one more round, one more meal, one less meal, or piece of candy, and it all adds up to gaining or losing that 5 pounds. Basically, you are a product of your environment. What you read and/or what you have listened to over the past 5 to 10 years has helped to shape who you are today. It didn't happen all at once, in just one day. Whatever you say or do right now is what makes you, you. If you take an extra bite of something, you will raise your insulin, and you will gain weight. It's that simple. So, there is no such thing as later. Right now, is what counts!

Every single moment in your life, you have only two options to choose from. The option of getting closer to your goal or getting further away from it. If you decide not to choose an option, you will not get closer by default. That's it. That is why having ownership of every single action in your life is so important because it is your life. Your life will not start Monday morning after the weekend is over. Your life is right now, and you have the control to make it better or worse right now, this very second. I'm not going to tell you what a good life looks like, that's up to you. I'm just making you aware of the fact that you are in control of creating it or not.

We all want temporary satisfaction to make us feel better. We all struggle with it. It's like the famous New Year's resolution. Everybody makes one, rarely does anybody keep to it. Temptations are too great, and the mind, as we have talked about before, likes to play little tricks on us to throw us off track. Like telling you that you've worked really hard last week, so you deserve a break and don't need to work as hard this week. That is so wrong! We all want to believe it, though, because we want to get away without the discomfort of pushing forward. That temporary satisfaction you get from that one potato chip or hanging in a bad company or buying that new pair of shoes is something we all struggle with. The fact of the matter is that there is no easy way. It all depends on how badly you want something.

When I meet with my clients for the first time, I ask them to paint me a picture of their typical daily routine. I want to see how they do things from the time they get up in the morning until they go to sleep at night. Do they read in the morning or at night? When and how do they wake up? Do they have a gratitude routine to start the day positively, or do they check social media first thing in the morning to fill their brains with garbage from the get-go? Do they eat a certain way or time? I want to hear what their daily routine looks like. I like to see if I can identify a trend that misaligns their routines with their goals.

I'll be honest, I don't really have a daily routine myself. I usually have to adjust my routine a lot to fit what is going on in my business. Here is what I learned. I do not schedule downtime. In workout communities, they talk about the "de-load" week. What you do is to schedule a week where you schedule downtime to let your body rest and recover a little bit. But I don't believe in this, and I don't do it. I find that it automatically happens by accident. What I mean is that clients cancel, plans change, things come up, and you find yourself with an unexpected block of time that you can fill with meditation or reading or something else. Or vice versa, things get so busy that I just don't have time to work out that week, and that becomes my de-load week. I work out when I am in between clients. It can be 30 minutes or an hour, whatever time is available to me. It can even be 3-hours on some days. It all depends on what is happening in my studio on that day. Whatever time I have available to me that day, I try to make the best out of it. However, I do schedule my business, my family time, and my spiritual practice. I will try to make everything else happen that I can, but these three things are non-negotiable. Working out is a must for me as well, it's my meditation and my sanity. But I don't schedule it because I work in a gym and usually I'll find at least half an hour for it at some point during the day. Otherwise I would most definitely schedule it as a must-do.

Most people think that since I work in a gym, workouts come easy to me. Yes, I do love working out. But when you spend 10 to 12 hours a day in a gym, working out can get old. I get tired and drained, just like you. And just like everyone else, I have to force myself to do the right thing even on rough days – because today counts and tomorrow could be even worse.

Sometimes I don't get home until 9:00 p.m. or 10:00 p.m. at night because of something crazy that was happening at my studio, and my kids and wife are already asleep. That's the sucky part of owning your own business. On most days, though, I feel so strongly that I need to be with my family that I somehow work it out to be home before they go to bed. I want to see them and be able to spend time with them and kiss them goodnight as often as possible. It's a sacrifice that I make because then I am up until 2:00 a.m. doing all the paperwork and answering emails for the business. Sometimes I'm running late, and I text my wife to see if they are still awake. When she texts me back that they are still awake, I am so happy. It means so much to me to be there. The 5 minutes at the end of a crazy busy day that I get to see them can take away all the frustration and sweat I have experienced the whole day. This is part of the 1% I talk about that all adds up to my being able to be successful in all things. Those times when I come home to kiss them all goodnight add up over time. They mean more than all the money I can make in a year or lifetime.

As for my routine - I try my hardest to make time for my family because they are my life. At least one day on the weekend I try to spend the whole day with them. For me, this is non-negotiable...PERIOD. I do not let anything interfere with family time. My family is the most important thing in my life. They support me and allow me to do this. I am nobody without them. I know of people who never even see their kids during the week. They have created no memories with them because they are so busy working. Time is short, and before you know it, your family will be grown and gone. I believe these people have lost sight of what is truly important, and it is something I cannot understand. I feel sad for them. So, I dedicate time to my family and give thanks for them every day. It is extremely difficult to balance a young growing business and a family life, but I am trying my absolute best here. Sometimes it just means that I have to sleep a little faster.

I believe that you start to crave things that you do consistently, right? I think that the more fitness you do, whether it's 20 or 40 minutes a day, the more you want to do it. Whether you are practicing your spiritual well-being or reading or improving your body, small gains add up. I am a big believer that your body, spirit, mind, and heart know exactly what is right for you and what will be wrong. It may be with your family, your business, your fitness or nutrition, whatever it is, you know deep inside the right thing to do. The more you do for yourself that is right, the more you will crave doing the right things. If you keep on doing the things that you know are wrong, the more you will keep craving the wrong things. This is the other important reason why you need to pay attention to all the small decisions and actions throughout the day. They will shape your habits, your cravings, and your mental momentum. It will strengthen or weaken your willpower. It's all about adjusting your actions. Adjust your actions, and your heart will follow. This goes back to one of my initial lessons about taking action, and the mind follows.

So here it is. Spending just 1% of your time or a few minutes every day, every week, or every month adds up. You cannot have a dollar without having one hundred cents. Whether it's being with your wife and kids, exploring your spirituality, running your business, or improving your body and health, small and continuous steps lead to greater success. Everything adds up! Everything counts! Right now, it is more important than tomorrow!

"The man who removes a mountain begins by carrying away small stones."

Chinese Proverb

BO'S HOMEWORK

Name 5 daily habits that seem insignificant yet sabotage your results negatively right now.

_____

_____

_____

_____

Name 5 small daily habits that you could incorporate to potentially get closer to your goal without spending too much time on them.

_____

_____

_____

_____

Chapter Ten

The Great Sabotage

This is a heavy topic for me because, as you read earlier, I am a procrastinator myself. But this is not just about me. I have already told you that I am at war with my inner procrastinator. It is about some of my clients, about some of you that are reading this book, about people that are struggling with taking control over their destiny, about the fear of change.

So many of my potential clients drive by my gym every day, thinking they should sign up but keep going. What happens while these people are procrastinating is, they get more out of shape, gain more weight, and their self-esteem keeps sliding lower and lower. It ends up preventing them from taking the first step they need to take because they know it will be even harder now. The longer they wait to take the

92

leap, the easier it becomes for them to talk themselves out of it. You want to know the funniest excuse I hear when I invite a potential client to try out our fitness program? People actually tell me that they aren't ready for me yet; that they need to get in shape first! Can you believe this? Believe it or not, I hear this excuse all the time. It's the number one excuse on the list! And every single time I hear it, I laugh! But you have to know that it drives me crazy! I just want to say to these people, "You do realize that this is what will get you into shape. This is what a trainer is for. This is my job, and I am here to help get you into shape." It's so contradictory. Of course, it's not easy. A workout is supposed to be a little challenging. Otherwise, you are literally wasting your time thinking that it will give you results. And I completely understand that it can be very intimidating to walk into a gym or fitness studio for the first time. But every single person there had to make that first step one day, and most people will always be super helpful as well as understanding. It goes back to your mind playing those little tricks on you to try to prevent you from doing the right thing, which can be uncomfortable.

To me, waiting to become better before you start is like nailing your own coffin shut. At some point, you won't be able to get out of it. It's like atrophying your muscles and mind. You will just continue to get weaker and spiral downward to the point where you can't bring yourself back up. You'll just stay in one place. Because atrophy exists, your cells will get weaker, your mind will get weaker, and your ability to take action will be lost. Look, when you don't move you don't progress. You lose any momentum you may have had, and your ability to do things will just get harder and harder until you just don't do them at all. Over time this will become the norm for you, rather than fixing it right away. We all know that it is easier to just sit back and not take any action than it is to step up and take responsibility, right? Because most of the time doing something and taking action is going to be hard.

It's really easy to lose desire. If you don't feel the desire, the fire will continue to get smaller and smaller and eventually burn out. I believe most people will desire something until it becomes too frustrating to achieve, so they just give up. How many people want a Land Rover or even a Lamborghini but lose their desire over time, give up and just drive the Civic or Corolla? I have to stop and give a little shout out to my clients that drive a Corolla or Civic and let them know that I am just using this example as an analogy, not a statement on their choice of cars. I myself drove a small Toyota Tercel when I first came to America. And that car was so bad you could see the pavement through the rusted floorboards. Anyway...

What this all comes down to is that you can't procrastinate. You are the one that fuels your own desires. If you desire something, you need to go after it. You can't let your mind play tricks on you and prevent you from going after what's right, after your dreams and goals. Anybody who keeps on driving past a gym and doesn't stop in, but complains about aches, pains or other health issues is going to eventually go into a state of paralysis in their life. The paralysis of staying in the same place, and not doing something causes your muscles to lose strength and your willpower to fade. This is going to sound rough, but have you ever seen people that just gave up and accepted a miserable existence without even putting up a fight? The hourglass is ticking down every day, no matter what. You need to understand that this chapter is not about working out or the gym. This chapter is about your life. About you standing up and taking control over your future right now. Waiting to do something will never serve you. If you don't take advantage now, you may not have time or strength later. It's your choice. What will you do?

"In a moment of decision, the best thing you can do is the right thing to do, the next best thing is the wrong thing, and the worst thing you can do is nothing."

Theodore Roosevelt

BO'S HOMEWORK

So here you are reading my book and thinking you should do "this."

_____

_____

_____

_____

So, why are you waiting? You cannot answer "for the time to be perfect."

_____

_____

_____

_____

Chapter Eleven

Rationalize the Negative, Visualize the Positive!

This is a big lesson here. We all understand that visualization can manifest a negative or positive outcome in anything you do, right? It's been around for a very long time. But it is worthy of discussion anytime you are taking important steps to improve your body or transforming your life.

Here is an example of something that happens in my studio all the time. There is what we call a box jump. You have probably seen or done it. Basically, there is a box, and your task is to jump on top of it. How you use your body to jump on the box is a test of your ability to generate power.

Now it's also a mind game for most people, not just a power exercise. When people just walk up to the box and try to jump on it but stop first, they fail. They get in front of it and can't seem to move. They can't move because they are thinking about it, and that generates fear. They become afraid that they won't be able to do it and that they could fail. The more they think about it, the less likely it is they will be able to do it. Essentially, they freeze. That's when I tell them to walk away from the box because they are thinking too much about it. I make them walk around the gym in a big circle and come back, but when they come back to the box, I tell them not to stop and just jump! Don't think, DO! Here's the thing. You can't do both. You can't stop in front of the box and jump at the same time. If you just act instead of thinking about it, it happens! What I have found, though, is that half of my clients will still walk up and stop. It's just not going to happen for them that day. Fear kicked in, and they can't seem to get past it, even though I know they are perfectly able to do it physically. The ones that actually listened to me are the successful ones. They just take the leap and go for it as they come around.

It all comes down to fear. It is called paralysis by analysis. A box jump is not a power exercise. It's a mindset exercise. The real power is to be able to see your vision and act upon it. You know that you can do it if you can visualize it.

If you visualize failure, you're going to fail. If you slip just a little and only give yourself the slightest chance of failure when you jump, you won't tuck your knees correctly, and your leap will fall short. You must always give a 100% commitment to something for it to happen. See yourself landing on that box. If you can't visualize yourself landing on the top of the box, you're going to land short. There is no negotiating this. It's like when you throw a ball. You have to keep your eyes on exactly where you want the ball to go when you execute your throw because as you release the ball, it will follow the path to wherever your eyes go. Make sense?

I had a lady here, a new client in the middle of a group class, and she jumped and missed the box. She was so embarrassed. She failed the first time, but she kept it up and eventually made it. Super proud of her, she did not give up! But when she was attempting it the first time before the class, she was totally fine and made it on the box. In class, she missed it because her overthinker kicked in. She was in front of other people, and that made her start to worry about what would happen if she failed. And trust me, everyone else was too out of breath to care. What she was doing was visualizing failing instead of succeeding. You can't do that! You can't visualize failure because you will fail. Or you fail because you don't put everything into it. Instead, you should be rationalizing the negatives. Meaning, ask the question,

"What's the worst that could happen?" For example, I'm going to try to jump on the box. The box is soft, so it's not going to break me, and I'll probably just roll off. The only thing that might really get hurt is my ego because I'm embarrassed. If I don't try at all I fail by default. It's a two-second rationalization that can turn your negative thoughts to positive and allow you to move on to visualizing making it! Or, you might decide from there that you should try a smaller box and build up your confidence before attempting the big box. Either way, you will take the negative to a positive place where you succeed.

The key here is to never put emotions into thinking about failure. Rationalize the negatives short, quick, and to the point. Then put your emotion into the visualization of success.

We all know that most people will see failure before they see success. What you need to do is to rationalize your fears of failure so that you can push out the negative thoughts. Understand that the fear is real and why you are feeling it, but don't let it overtake you. Then you will be able to get it out of the way and in turn, visualize your success. Every single one of my clients that have done this and succeeded will be reading my book and telling you that this is true! Always "Rationalize the negative and visualize the positive!"

"If you can dream it, you can do it."

Walt Disney

BO'S HOMEWORK

Are you allowing negative thoughts to prevent you from achieving great things?

_____

_____

_____

Take a negative thought about starting your fitness program and visualize what you will look and feel like after a month, two months…

_____

_____

_____

Next time you are afraid to take action towards your goal, think about the worst-case scenario and how it will affect your life. Then visualize the perfect outcome and how that makes you feel. Which is greater?

_____

_____

_____

Chapter Twelve

The Only Short Cut

In the very beginning, I did everything by myself and man, oh man, did I make mistakes! I spent so much money on insisting that I learn my own lessons. I didn't look for guidance from others who may have already been through it. Oh, I learned my lessons. But I sure made it hard on myself, and I wasted a lot of time and money doing it that way. I'm talking about losing thousands of dollars before I woke up to this idea of learning from others. Now the first thing I tell people is that the only short cut is to learn from someone who has already done it. Why would you make your own mistakes if you can learn from someone else's?

I am a firm believer in listening. If someone has something to say and their track record speaks for them, I shut up and listen. It's a very good idea. You don't gain anything from talking. You've probably heard the expression, "you have two ears and only one mouth for a reason." Everyone teaches you how to speak. We teach it at home and in schools and colleges. But nobody is teaching anyone about how to listen. And it's so much more important. Just shut up and listen, and you'll be amazed at what you can learn!

I know most of my strengths and weaknesses, which, by the way, is the biggest thing for an entrepreneur to learn. One of those was trying to do it all myself when there are so many people out there that teach about these things I screwed up on every day. I can point you in the direction of many books and mentors that share their experiences, and I tell you they have already done most of what I was able to screw up on my own. Think about how much aggravation and frustration I could have avoided if I had been willing to find out and take advantage of what these folks were more than willing to share with me?

There are many famous and successful people out there to learn from in any aspect of life. Thought leaders like Tony Robbins, Grant Cardone, and Robert Kiyosaki are obviously some of the influencers I listened to at the beginning of my journey. I love to learn from former navy seals like Jocko Willink, Robert O'Neill, and David Goggins and their life lessons. Books by Brian Tracy, Michael Gerber, and Donald Miller were also extremely helpful in building my business.

There are also Podcasts by Ed Mylett, Gary Vaynerchuk, Andy Frisella, Tom Bilyeu, and many more that I love to learn from. And I still listen to my former business mentor Tim Lyons. There are so many other incredibly smart and successful people I have learned from over the years. So, this is my shout out to them because they have shared their mistakes and successes with me so I can avoid the pitfalls that slow me down. Almost all of this knowledge is free. So if somebody ever tells me that they don't know how to do something, I just hear that it's not important enough for them to know.

When I go to networking events, I have a hard time walking up to people to connect. I love to connect to good people, but so much of my energy is taken up by flipping the switch with my clients that it seems to dampen my ability to make myself show up at these events. I do it because I know I have to, but I am not as much of an extravert there as it might seem from my advertising and classes I teach. It takes a lot to flip the switch when there's like 15 people in my class waiting for me to help them flip their own switch. It takes so much energy because I always have to be "on" with them. And I have only so much energy to give, so when I walk into these events, I have to really force myself to flip my switch back on so I can get in front of these people to network. It's not that I don't want to, it's just that I have already given up a lot of my energy to my clients and business.

The thing is you can learn lessons from people that are not famous too. I learn from my clients every single day when they present me with their challenges. I find myself trying to create the best scenarios for helping them, and by taking that action, I learn something new at the same time. It's kind of a weird experience to know that even though I am a certified trainer and even have a degree in this, I can still learn from teaching others. It's kind of a weird concept, but when you are creating lessons for others, you are also creating lessons for yourself.

Everything is connected to everything in life. The laws of physics say that energy is transferrable. Everything in life you do will transform into movement or into heat. And making it hot is pretty cool too. When I was in my early teens, I looked up to my uncle. He was into multimedia production and a music video creator. Now he makes his own films. But I would sit and watch him edit, and from there, I learned to edit. Now, I am not a pro editor, but I can tell you that the things I learned from my uncle have given me the ability to put together some awesome videos for my social media ads. This skill has nothing to do with fitness, but it is a skill that I can use to help my fitness business grow. It connects me to potential clients in a better way.

I was also a musician at one time. I traveled across Eastern Europe with various bands. But then I met my lovely wife, and as you can see, I'm no longer a traveling musician. The point here is that, although being a musician has little to do with fitness, it does help my fitness business. I use it in my ads to help generate business and revenue. I also use it to keep the rhythm and energy in my classes upbeat. I use it as a motivational tool for my clients. Every single second of any of my classes has a specific song designed to keep the energy up and people motivated. I operate it with a remote. If I'm talking, I turn the music down. Sometimes the music is played at a little higher volume to create a higher level of energy. If someone is struggling, I start pumping up the beat and turn the music up a little louder to give them an extra push. Again, it's all connected.

My ability to help someone change their life gives me the motivation to make them try harder and push themselves. Underneath all this, my family is always on my mind, inspiring me and reminding me of my purpose for doing this. They are the ones that make me get up early to make those calls and close those deals so that my business continues to grow. They force me into action and learning as much as I can so that I can put 100% into what I have created. People are my inspiration. People ask me how I can do this with a family and what I say to them, I would not been able to do it without one!

Without them, it wouldn't really matter to me if I failed. But if my kids don't eat, it's my fault. So, I better figure things out, pronto!

This isn't just about fitness, either. You can use this technique for anything you want to do. Whether you want to be a marriage counselor, lawyer, lose weight, or anything else. The point to all of this is that there are people out there that have done it before you. And these people are more than willing to share their mistakes and things they did right with you. All you have to do is to listen and learn so that you don't have to go through the same mess getting to your vision. It's the only shortcut you can take that will help you to get where you want to be faster and easier than they had it. And the lessons you take away from these people will be invaluable to you if you are willing to take advantage of them.

"Wisdom is not a product of schooling but of the lifelong attempt to acquire it."

Albert Einstein

BO'S HOMEWORK

Are you trying to start a new project on your own?

_____

_____

_____

_____

Have you taken the time to read books or other forms of information by people that have already done it?

_____

_____

_____

_____

Are you willing to invest in a mentor that can help you get there quicker by sharing the mistakes they've already made with you?

_____

_____

_____

_____

Chapter Thirteen

It's All About the Whole Package

Every single day I see people come into my studio. I see all these white eyes looking back at me to change their lives. That is a huge responsibility! And, their energy sometimes transfers onto me. One might be having a bad day, the other could be pissed off at their spouse, or maybe they work for a bad boss. Whatever it is, I can't let it affect my energy and purpose. When I flip the switch to on, it has to stay on, and I go with it. So, I keep my cool and focus purely on serving them. Through serving, I push out the negativity, and it's then that I can feel the change in everyone. When we are done, I feel accomplished, and everyone wins.

112

This fitness industry is a very hard industry to be in. Every single person I serve, which is every half an hour, has a different energy. Whether it's with individuals or a class with 10 to 15 people, I get bombarded throughout the day, and I need to adapt and change up my energy 20 or 30 times during that day. Throughout the day, I find that my thermostat is setting and resetting depending on the people around me and what is going on. I am constantly adjusting it up or down to create the energy levels required for my individual client's needs. It can be overwhelming. But at the end of the day, I have to keep the switch on until every last client has left the studio. Then, BOOM! I collapse! And I think, holy moly, I did it! That's when I sit down for 30 minutes to gather myself up and find myself again. You always need to get back to who you are. Getting back to that safe place that brings you peace of mind is what allows you to continue to bring good energy to your clients. Who I am, what I am about and what I do to adapt to all of these people every day is draining. Yet, when a client comes back the next day and thanks me for what I am doing for them, it really lifts me up, and I think, "Wow! This is okay. This is why I do this." Now I have the energy for the next 30 clients, and I am going with it!

I am so thankful that I am able to serve. That I have a purpose in life and can make money at it too. You see, for me, it's not all about the money, it's my motivation to change lives.

The money will come and go, but when a client thanks me for sticking with them even when they were difficult and helping them to fix their body and life, my anxiety goes away, and I am on top of the world.

In the big picture, we all pretty much have the same goal. We want freedom; we want to have the opportunity for a great life with good relationships. If we stay healthy, we have longevity. We all have the same goals, really. The way we accomplish them and what our success looks like is different. But the big picture is the same for everyone. I feel my goal throughout the day is to pull people from one or another direction to bring them back to center, to the big picture. Everyone I work with is going in a different direction. I feel that it is my job to pull or push them toward their big-picture goals and the vision they have for themselves. At the end of the day we all want what makes us happy. When people hire you as a coach, they aren't looking to just lose five pounds. What they are really looking for is to have the energy to live a better life and be happy. They want to be able to play with their kids, grandkids, take vacations to faraway places, and enjoy it.

It's never about the five pounds. It's about happiness and where you find it. So, you spend your life raising your kids and doing all the things you need to do to support and raise the family. Then one day, the kids are gone off to college, and the two of you are looking at each other with nothing to say.

The everyday obligations of raising your family have been the center of your universe all these years, and you've both lost sight of yourselves through all the sacrifices you've made. You may be looking at each other and seeing each other differently. Like she let herself go, and he's been way too busy working because you needed money for the kid's college. You realize suddenly that you've grown apart, and in completely different directions. Because she was so focused on kids, she forgot to take care of herself. She didn't pay attention to her body or health, and now she's lost her confidence. And you lost your connection with her because you've been too busy at work to care about her.

So, she shows up at my studio and tells me she thinks she needs to lose 10 or 15 pounds. NO! Let's move, let's change it! I tell her what we really need to do is to get your confidence back and make you believe in yourself again. The weight loss is merely a side effect of regaining your sense of self and being happy again. She has new-found friends at the gym, and she is standing taller, walking with confidence. She can move and keep up. Suddenly her husband is noticing her again and appreciating what he sees. He's interested and wants to do things together again. He also starts getting nervous about her new confidence and appearance, to the point where he is starting to pick himself up again as well.

They start growing together and finding new common interests.

You see, this was just a simple example, one of the things I see every day. But when I work with clients, it's never about just losing the 5 lbs. When they start to see the results, they stand taller and feel more confident in themselves, they realize it's about the inside. It's about bringing their vision of happiness back to life. It's about creating new energy and being able to move. It's all connected, as I said before. One cup spills into one part of your life that spills into another part of your life, and so on. So many times have I seen this, where one family member starts working out with me and the next thing you know the whole family is getting into health and fitness. It's all a big lesson. If you learn one thing it will filter down into everything you do in life. Look, every human craves the same things in one shape or another. It may start with fitness but ultimately transfers to every part of your life. You might start out with the idea that you want to lose 5 or 10 pounds, but it will always end up with the changing of your life, better family relationships, and being more engaged in your community.

I have a client who struggled mightily when she first came to me. Now, I have a lot of clients that struggle with anxiety, but this one was the latest one that is standing out in my memory right now. There were instances in the beginning when she came into the studio without a smile. Her face was in total anguish. I'd see her hands shaking uncontrollably, and she would have this robotic look on her face. She was so afraid of me, or maybe even life in general, I was never sure what might happen. Some days she would come in all hunched over and tell me she just couldn't do it, then run back out and just sit in her car. She just couldn't do anything. How can a person have so much anxiety, I thought?

It turned out that her doctor had been telling her to start working out to relieve her anxiety. But she was one of those that kept on driving by and never stopping. Then one day, her body just picked her up and dragged her in before she could think about it. She started to move, and everything just fell into place. What happens when you create action and start to move, that movement creates hormones. And hormones create the power for decision making. So, she did the right thing. Now, after 6 months of working with her, she comes in smiling and high-fives me. I am so proud of her. I am proud that she is actually taking action and fighting for a better self! She brings her husband with her, and he has told me so many times how grateful he is for this decision. I ask him what he means, and he tells me every time she comes home from her workouts, she is smiling. She's a new person. BOOM! That's my purpose! Fortunately, or unfortunately, I have so many of these stories.

Right now, I want to thank all of my clients for giving me purpose. My family gives me motivation. My clients give me purpose. It's ridiculous! I mean, I've gone from lifting dumbbells to changing and even saving lives. It's unbelievable.

STAY SORE!

"If you light a lamp for someone else, it will also brighten your path."

Buddha

BO'S HOMEWORK

Think hard about what your real goal is? I'm sure you want to lose weight or make some extra money, but what is the real reason?

Write it down!

_____

_____

_____

_____

_____

_____

_____

_____

_____

_____

_____

_____

Chapter Fourteen

How Bad Do You Want It

Every decision in life, every success or failure, comes down to one question: "How bad do you want it?"

I have an older client that started working out with me over 4 years ago. When we first started, she was already retired and kept asking me if she is too old to workout. Of course, I told her that the older you are, the more important working out becomes. Her physical strength, endurance, and overall fitness improved tremendously in the last four years we have worked together. She keeps telling me that she would have never believed this to be possible, and she keeps telling everyone else that they should work out no matter what age they are. In the beginning she would get out of breath just walking into the gym. Fast forward a few years, and she finished second in a 5K for her age class. But she would never listen to me when I would talk about nutrition. Almost every session I would tell her that I can make her stronger, but she needs to eat right in order to change her body composition more dramatically. I am not a nutritionist. Therefore, I would only talk about general principles of nutrition and give her guidelines and ideas. She would always nod and agree but never actually do anything about it. Well, until now.

About half a year ago, she went to get her physical, and her blood sugar tests were concerning. Her doctor said that she is borderline diabetic, and if she keeps eating the way she is eating right now she might have to start taking insulin shots. Can you imagine how badly that scared her? Taking a needle to your stomach and/or finger every single day for the rest of your life. Obviously besides the needle there are other health implications associated with diabetes. But that needle thing really scared her! Long story short, she lost over 45 pounds since then. Turns out, the doctor gave her the exact same nutrition principles I was talking about for years. Which means that she had the tools all along but didn't want to use them? Today she is lean, strong and healthy. Almost always, no matter what it is, it is possible. You just need to want it bad enough!

I'm sure you have heard about stories where a mother lifts a car off her baby or fights a wild animal to protect her child. How is that even possible? The answer is simple. That mother has a strong enough reason!

This is going to sound rough, but it will get the point across, I hope. Imagine this situation. Imagine a trainer tells his client to do two more squats, and the client says that he can't because he is too exhausted. If you put a gun against his head and say two more, he will most definitely find the strength to do so. Again, it always comes down to your inner deeper reason. It comes down to how bad you want something.

Many people in general and many of my own clients keep telling me they don't have time to eat right, they don't have time to track their food, they don't have time to work out, they can't stop smoking, they can't eat "cardboard tasting" boring food, they can't eat vegetables because they taste yucky... Until something bad happens. Your first heart attack or bypass surgery, and you have all the time in the world to take care of your health. The first insulin shot needle, and all of a sudden, the idea of eating vegetables is not that bad anymore. The moment your doctor tells you to do a test to rule out cancer, that's the moment where quitting smoking doesn't seem that impossible anymore. All it takes is a strong enough reason, and everything becomes possible.

I do not judge my clients or any other person's decision. It is your life and your decision! Who am I to tell you what you want?! But I do need you to say it how it is! Instead of saying this is too hard, say it's not important enough. Instead of saying I don't have time for this, just say it's not important enough for me to find the time. Instead of finding excuses, just say out loud that longevity is not that important to you. Instead of saying I am poor, just say I don't want to work harder. Instead of saying I was not as lucky as the next person, just say I didn't create as many opportunities as the next person. Instead of saying she has great genetics, just say I'm not willing to do what she is doing.

All right, this next part that I am going to talk about is not about a specific person. When some of my clients are going to read this, they are going to think it's specifically about them, but this is probably about 20 or 30 percent of the people that come to my gym.

Imagine for a second that you are in my position, that you are the trainer, and you want your clients to have great and visible results. You ask your client if they exercised yesterday, and they say "no" because work was too hectic, and things just got crazy, and they had no time to work out whatsoever. And then the rest of the work out they talk to you about yesterday's Game of Thrones episode and how epic it was. I hope you see where I am going with this. I know that everything I say sounds very black and white, very robotic, mechanical, and not fun at all. But in reality it doesn't have to be… give it some color. Let me give you my own example. This might sound funny, but it is very true. I watched the entire first season of Game of Thrones while I was working out. I had two cheap adjustable dumbbells and a rusty barbell I had purchased from Craigslist. I couldn't afford a gym membership back then, and I didn't have a TV, so I set up my phone in one corner of the room and worked out while streaming the show. One episode equaled one workout; where there is a will, there is a way.

If you want something, take it. If you are not taking it, you don't want it bad enough. Achievements don't have to be boring and colorless. Be creative. Find a workout that is actually fun. Try different spices for your vegetables. If you need money, find something you're passionate about and then work doesn't feel like work anymore. If you don't have time, then condense it. If you want it bad enough, you will find a way.

"Some people want it to happen, some wish it would happen, others make it happen."

Michael Jordan

BO'S HOMEWORK

What's holding you back from achieving your dream?

_____

_____

_____

_____

Review your priorities. Do your priorities resemble how bad you want it?

_____

_____

_____

_____

How much are you willing to put into your dream so that you can accomplish it?

_____

_____

_____

_____

Chapter Fifteen

Less Can Be More

More is not always better! Many of my clients are looking for what else they should do to get the results they want. Nine times out of ten, the answer is that they should be doing less. They should be eating less and working out less. Eating less is actually less work, therefore even simpler than eating more. Some of them want to lose weight so badly that they come to eight classes during the week. Well, there are only seven days to work out. Doing eight workouts during the week is not going to help them. We need to give our bodies time to react and adapt to our workouts. So, you should really be working out less! You need to give your body time to recover, rebuild, and restore muscle and energy. If you keep overdoing it, your body is going to break down because you

128

haven't given it the time it needs to rest. You'll end up hurting yourself more than helping yourself in the end.

This can be applied to all areas of your life. If you are in business and you're running around in a million different directions like I did when I started, you lose sight of your focus. I was trying to start my website and do social media and sell to my potential clients, and the list goes on. That kept me from focusing on the really important things, and certain things that needed to get done were naturally missed. All because I ended up focusing too much in one area and neglecting another. Then things began to fall apart in all areas.

Think about relationships. When you are young, and you are looking for a lady; say you find one you really like. If you constantly text and call her over and over, she's going to get annoyed. This kind of behavior is smothering her and puts her off. But, if you back off a bit and keep your distance a little, she's probably going be intrigued. She'll want to get to know you because there is some mystery there and she'll start to want some attention. Again, less can be more...

I always teach my clients to do less volume with more intensity. I want them to keep their workouts short, intense, and focus on the important stuff. Instead of squeezing in 10 things, I want them to do 3 things really well. That's how they become better. Look, if you work out for an hour a day, it doesn't mean you will become better by increasing your workout to 2 hours a day or 3 hours a day. It's not a good use of your time. So, I always teach my clients to focus on less volume but more intensity. Doing your routine right means becoming better at fewer things that make the biggest difference and bring the best results early on rather than trying to do everything all at once. Work out so intense that you can't possibly work out the following day. That tells me you did it right, and you don't have to waste your time every single day in the gym. But the problem is most people don't want to be that uncomfortable and just want to be on cruise control when working out. And then I have to hear how they work out every day but still don't see results. I don't care how many times you do something, I care about how much heart you put into it!

We all have a life to live. Let's say you're trying to take on too many projects with your business. If you keep adding more and more and more to your plate, you're eventually going to lose sight of something, and something important will be forgotten. It comes back to seeking discomfort and setting priorities. Usually, if you are trying to do 10 things, seven of them are probably not all that important, but they are easy. Then there are three that you know you have to do but aren't really into because they are uncomfortable, or you don't like to do them. You already know that I write everything down. So, when I write down all the things I need to do, I set the priorities for the 10 tasks I think I have to accomplish. Then I rank them from most important to least important. This way I can quickly recognize that 7 of them were just artificially created to avoid the discomfort of doing the 2 or 3 that need to get done.

Seek the discomfort and get the 2 or 3 hard tasks out of the way. Then you can go home feeling like you've really accomplished something that is important to growing your business or whatever it is you are trying to improve in life. Or keep your relationship on track and manage your life. This act of accomplishment actually produces those hormones I talked about that are going to help change your body instead of just goofing around with light dumbbells and making enough sweat to say you did something. Always work on getting the uncomfortable, heavy lifting out of the way first. Everything else will follow.

I will caution you here, though. Don't forget about resting and recharging in all of this. It's very easy when you are running around at a hundred miles an hour to forget that you need to stop and rest now and then. Rest is a very important component of balancing your life and activities. Think about your own smartphone. It's not going to keep going indefinitely. You need to recharge it now and again to keep it running, right? This is true for you and me, as well.

Here is a good example of what I mean. Last year I was running my business really hard. I was trying to do everything in my power to make this business work and feel like a great and trustworthy place for my clients. I hadn't yet figured out that I needed somebody to teach me business, so I was doing it all on my own. Anyway, on this one day, I found myself with some time to slow down. Two of my clients had canceled back to back, and I gained an hour of time all to myself. The gym was quiet and empty, and I sat down for a minute. But then something weird happened. I had gone through my day as I do, training clients and working out and I was feeling good. Things were going along normally when all of a sudden, out of nowhere, I started to breathe heavily and felt my heart start pounding like it was going to come right out of my chest. I was scared! I started thinking this is it, here I am 30 years old, and I'm having a heart attack!

So, I went out to my car and drove myself, not to the emergency hospital, but to the pharmacy, so I could check my blood pressure on their machine (I have a blood pressure cuff in the gym now). And my blood pressure was through the roof, something like 180/120. I got a little nervous, so I drove myself straight away to the Urgent Care. No, not the emergency room, the Urgent Care. It was closer… Anyway, I told the girl at the desk that I couldn't breathe and needed to see someone right away, that it was getting worse. So, she got me to sit down right away. They immediately did an EKG to check my heart. When they finished, they told me that the results showed I had one of the strongest hearts they had seen. It was working like perfection. Now I was confused. But they told me that there was absolutely nothing wrong with my heart and that I did not have a heart attack. Whew! But what was it?

They asked a lot of questions, and I told them that I don't smoke, I don't drink, and I make sure I eat correctly. I was honest and let them know that I did drink a little caffeine because I'm a businessperson, and I work like 25 hours a day most of the time. 25 is not a typo. That's when the doctor asked me to let her see my schedule. She wanted to know what I was doing throughout my day. So, I pulled out my phone and showed it to her. She just shook her head and said, "Yeah, looking at this, you're going to be back here within two months with the same problem." Basically, she told me that I was having an extremely strong stress-related panic attack due to a high level of anxiety and stress! She told me that I needed to figure out how to balance my life better and learn to take a step back now and then. Well, first of all, I cannot tell you the relief I felt at that moment. Because I really thought I was going to maybe die of a heart attack, that's how bad it felt.

It turns out that constantly going a hundred miles an hour all the time without resting and allowing myself to recharge had created the perfect environment for my body and mind to overcompensate and then crash. I didn't know any better. I was trying so hard to become successful. Going a hundred miles an hour was great because it kept me from becoming anxious and worrying. At least at the surface. But you can't sustain that for long before it all catches up to you. I was so focused on my success that I never gave myself time to stop and recharge. Hey, even race car drivers bring their cars in for pit stops every so many laps around the racetrack. We should all be doing the same. Every so often, you need to take time for a pit stop. Step back, reevaluate where you came from and where you are going. Drink some water and allow your body to relax a little and your mind to reset. Recharge and then go hard and fast again till the next pit stop. That's how you win the race.

Rest is so important. Part of less being more is to understand that by doing too much too often, you are not giving your body and mind enough time to rest and to recharge. Whether it's physical, mental, financial or just allowing your mind and body to breathe, you need to recharge to be able to continue to operate effectively. Part of doing less is what allows you to gain more. Setting aside time to let yourself recharge can help to open and expand your mind's ability to view problems from a different angle. It gives you an opportunity to take a fresh look at things, which then helps you see solutions you might not have seen before.

Part of what I have learned while creating my business is that you sometimes have to just step back and look at all you've accomplished so far. I say I learned, but really, I am still learning to do this. It's important because I can get so carried away with all these crazy ideas of mine. I start thinking about email campaigns and hiring trainers and growing the business. Sometimes I get frustrated because I have so much more that I need to do. It becomes overwhelming, and I start to feel negative thoughts come in telling me it won't work out, and I'm going to fail. All the things I've been telling you that you should not let happen. Remember, "rationalize the negative and visualize the positive!"

What I found really helps me out now is to just take a step back for 2 or 3 days every 4 to 6 months and just allow myself to recharge. I know it's not much, but it's a start. I should do it for 2 or 3 weeks, but that would just make my anxiety go to a whole other level. Anyway, I take these 2 or 3 days, and I don't look at my website, I don't check email or social media. I don't plan anything new for the business. I just take time to reflect on what I have accomplished so far. I take out pictures that I have been taking since I started out and look at them. I have this one that I am most fond of, where I

135

am just sitting on the floor of my studio when it wasn't covered. The whole room is empty, the floor is cement, and I am just dreaming of what it is going to become. It's a wow moment for me every time because I can see how far the business has come. Then I pick up some of my notepads from 2016 when I started and look at all the goals I had listed then. Some have gone well, some not. But I can see what I have built, and it puts everything back into perspective.

To sum it all up, it's more important to do the three uncomfortable and hard things than it is to waste your time on seven unimportant tasks that don't produce results. I've learned that you can't muscle through everything and taught myself to take a step back now and again. I understand now why less is often more, and I teach this to my clients. Go hard, get uncomfortable, do what's challenging yet most important, and then step back to appreciate the results of your hard labor. What I know is that you can't do everything! In the end, it catches up with you. Therefore spend your energy wisely and direct your momentum towards your priorities. What would happen to my family or my clients if I was not here for them? Well, if I do not take care of myself, then I cannot take care of them. I owe it to them and myself to become the best version of myself so that I can help them to become the best version of themselves. Doing less really does result in more if you direct your intensity in the right direction. Doing more is for lazy people that are not willing to go hard on the important stuff.

"Focus on being productive instead of busy."

Tim Ferriss

BO'S HOMEWORK

Take a minute to think about your usual routine throughout the day. List 3 things you could do less of, which in turn would get you closer to your goals.

_____

_____

_____

_____

Chapter Sixteen

Set Loud Goals!

The easiest person to lie to is yourself. I have a hard time comprehending how easy it is for people to lie to themselves and believe it. So, they set their goal to run 2 miles every day. Then they go out and do it the first day. But the next day they only run 1.5 miles. They tell themselves it is just for this one time. Then the next thing you know, they've come up with another excuse to not even run the next day. They keep coming up with excuses to convince themselves it's okay. Eventually, they just don't do anything.

Setting loud goals means making a LOUD and BOLD statement that lets everybody know this is what I will do, and this is going to happen! It sets the expectation that you can expect me to do this! It's putting pressure on yourself to do and give it your all!

Let me give you a simple example. I train people that compete in bodybuilding, physique, or bikini shows. When clients tell me they want to lose 15 pounds in three months, I will guarantee you that in three months most of them will still be wanting to lose 15 pounds. That's just how it works. But if they post this on social media and then register for a show, they let everyone know that they are doing this, then it will happen. Why? Because now they have put themselves up on stage for everyone to see and if they don't do it, they will look like a fool. If they don't do what needs to get done today, everything they talked about doesn't count. We talked about this before, every little percent that you do counts.

Basically, when you declare yourself and your goals loud and proud, you're putting it all out to the Universe. And the Universe is going to hold you accountable. Stating your intentions to the world in front of other people automatically makes you accountable. You feel it inside. You're staking your bond and reputation on making it happen. If you don't come through, you will lose your credibility and your reputation with other people. People aren't going to think much of your word after that because you didn't follow through with your actions. They're going to think, if you can't hold your promise to your own self, how will you be able to honor your commitment to others.

It's easy to lie to yourself, right? We all do it. But when you shout out to the world these big and bold intentions, you can't really get away with lying to yourself. When you set your intentions with the world watching, you are giving yourself a deadline and telling them exactly what you expect the results to be. Maybe you're going to write a book by 2020 or create a new fitness habit by the end of the year. It's a specific goal with a deadline attached to it.

What I tell my clients is that when you set a LOUD goal, you leave no room for interpretation. You need to be clear and specific about what your goal is, and you need it to be as simple as possible so that nobody can imagine it to be something different than what your intent really is. You don't get to move the target to a different day because you've already set your deadline. It doesn't matter if it's losing 20 pounds, releasing your first book, meeting a financial goal. It has to be something so specific that no one will misunderstand it. The more specific you are, the more it counts -- every day, every hour, every minute, and every rep counts! If you're going to be on stage in a two-piece bikini that probably only has four ounces of fabric in it, you are going to make every single rep you do stand out.

It's like auto training. The more you shout it out to the world, the more your consciousness starts to process it and works to make it happen. It's like when you are constantly around negative people, it rubs off, and you're going to become negative. When you surround yourself with positive people, you stay positive. If you say to yourself 100 times that you are stupid, you're going to start feeling stupid. But if you tell yourself 100 times that you are going to achieve your goal, you will achieve your goal. It's a very simple concept, but it's how things work. It's all about creating good habits and staying true to your promises and to yourself. When you shout to the world you are going to do this you are making a commitment and letting the universe hold you accountable to getting it done. Whatever you are committed to achieving, when you say it out loud to others, you most probably will.

If you are doing these things for someone else, your loved ones, for instance, there is so much more pressure to succeed, right? It's a good thought. My wife and family and my clients give me purpose. They keep me accountable to my goals even when I think I want to give up sometimes.

So, my loudest goal was the one I set when I stated that I was going to start my own fitness business. The fitness business is interesting because gyms are almost always started by former athletes. Some played college football or were wrestling champions, you know. And here I was, a nobody! I came here with a dream, and I didn't know anyone. I never had played in an organized sports game or on a team in my life. When people ask me what sport I played in school, I always told them that I played guitar. I had no connections and no idea how to open a business. Especially in an industry run by sports heroes. In Ukraine, we don't have football. We don't have baseball. In our school, we had one soccer ball for the whole school, and the teacher would have to make sure everyone got a fair chance to play with it. So, when my clients would talk about football, I had no idea what was going on or what they were talking about. All I knew was there was a Cleveland team. That's it!

Opening a fitness gym was really such a crazy idea because the people who were opening gyms were all these ex-college athletes. They knew all the people I didn't know. I had nothing to go on except for my dream. What I did know was that I loved the human body and that I could help people. That's it. Now people call me Dr. Bo because I give them help without pills and provide them with natural ways to improve their bodies and lives. I encourage them to eat healthily and give them exercise programs that make them feel and look better.

One of the reasons I started my own business was because I had worked in a big box gym, and I had such a reputation that 5 other gym owners had approached me at varying times about working for them as a trainer. That's when I started to think to myself, well, if all these people believe in me this much and they all want me to do this, maybe, just maybe I have what it takes to do it for myself. Maybe I can make up for not being a recognized athlete and my lack of connections in the fitness world by hustling more, reading more, and my desire to help other human beings succeed in meeting their fitness goals. So, I set my own LOUD GOAL! Which, when I look back, made no sense at the time.

In fitness, social media is a good way of broadcasting a loud goal. Social media works as a tool for maintaining accountability. Think about bikini and figure competition. A figure competitor that is preparing for competition has to make every day count. Every single meal has to be weighed and logged because the competition is coming up in 16 weeks, and messing up only one meal could be the difference between first and last place. So, every day for her counts, and she needs to stay completely focused on the goal because the competition is coming up.

It could be different things too. I have another female client that wants to be able to squat 225 lbs. She's a really strong girl, and she's trying to get there. The problem is that she only tells her goal to me. I keep telling her that she should be sharing her goal with everyone she knows so that they can help her stay accountable to the goal. But she still only tells me.

Business is another area where you should be setting loud goals. Money, although necessary, I don't personally

145

care for it, is another loud goal you can set for your business. How much money should you plan to make in the first year, the second year, etc.?

When I was mentoring with Tim Lyon's, we had to set some goals, and I was always very uncomfortable talking about money. To me, it is just a way of exchanging value, and I have a hard time with that. But I am learning that it can be helpful if you treat it right. You can help people with money. The more money you have, the more you can help and actually impact others!

Whether a person is going to be judged on stage or whether it's the business of writing a book and putting your story out to people, you're going to be judged. You are going to be judged in anything that you do. So, whether you're judged on social media, in person, or at your business, you can gain strength from it. Whatever gives you the ability and strength to just get better is great! I know people that read this right now are probably saying to themselves that this idea of putting yourself out there is a little too rough! You have to be comfortable getting vulnerable once in a while. Being vulnerable can be a strength that you can use to your advantage if you're smart. If you open yourself up and not let yourself be afraid of failing, just say, "Hey, I'm going to do this to the absolute best of my ability!" you'll crush it!

Making yourself accountable is the most important thing about setting loud goals. Take a minute to say your goal out loud. Now watch as everyone around you suddenly starts to check out whether you're going to make it or not. You have put your intentions out there, and everyone is going to work to help hold you accountable for reaching that goal!

"Accountability breeds responsibility."

Stephen R. Covey

BO'S HOMEWORK

Think of your goals.

Which one is most important to you?

_____

_____

_____

_____

Are you willing to put it out there so the world can hold you accountable?

_____

_____

_____

_____

Chapter Seventeen

GPS Your Goals

So, we've talked a lot about setting goals. But now you've got to map out how you are going to get there. That is what I call GPSing the goals. When you log into your GPS, there are certain criteria you have to put into the program so that it can map out your direction and get you to the right place. Number one, obviously, you put in your goal destination. But your GPS also has to know where you are right now in order to create the path. You have to be very truthful about where you are now, or your directions will be fumbled. If you lie to yourself and set an unrealistic starting point, it's going to be much harder to get where you want, and you may even wind up in a bad place.

Now that you have set your starting point and you have determined what your finish line looks like, you have to deal with the hard work in between. In the GPS settings, you can set your preferences for how you get to your destination. When you think about it, it's the same exact thing you would have to choose in real life. If you want to get to your goals as fast as possible, you can use the fastest route by time. You might have to pay for tolls, but you'll get there faster. That's the same as paying a professional to help you get to your goals faster. For Example when you are sick, you go to a doctor. When you want to become fit, you go to a trainer. When you are having relationship problems you go to a counselor. Or when you have legal issues you go to a lawyer.

Also, in a GPS you can choose to use the shortest route by distance. It might not be the fastest, but you'll spend less money on gas and maintenance on the vehicle. The same goes for real-life goals. If you don't have much money to spend on your goals, at least research the fastest way to get there organically. Money is not always the only solution to a problem. You can read books, watch lectures or find forums online that will guide you to your goals for free. A GPS has options for everyone. If you are afraid of high-speed traffic, quick decision and high risk, you can always choose to avoid highways altogether. That's an option in your GPS settings as well. You will get there much slower but stress-free.

So, as you see, you have to choose your starting point and finish line very carefully, otherwise you will never get to your goal destination. And after that, you have to decide which driving style fits you best. Or, in other words, how are you willing to drive to get there the fastest?

And now, probably the most important part about GPSing your goals. A GPS has to always keep track of your location, where you are right now. That way, it can always tell you when to switch lanes, when to slow down and when the next turn comes up. In order to get you to your goal, the GPS has to always know where you are at this very moment and keep track of your movements at all times. This principle applies to absolutely everything in life, especially achieving goals and being successful!

If you want to lose weight, you obviously have to track your nutrition intake. Otherwise, you won't know when to switch lanes, when to take a turn, and even what route to use. How can you possibly know how to adjust your nutrition when you don't know what nutrition you are getting?

When you run a business, you have to have a detailed accounting in order to understand where your expenses are coming from and where most of your profits are generated. That's the only way to predict how future decisions impact your business. You have to have daily, weekly, and monthly reports and spreadsheets in order to know what marketing techniques are working, where the most revenue is coming from, which investments have the most return, which strategies perform most efficiently, and so on. You have to keep track of your business at all times, or you won't know if you are lost. The same goes for relationships, spirituality, health and everything else you can possibly imagine. Figure out how you can keep track of your progress. Otherwise you won't even know when you get lost.

I am the GPS for my clients. Again, when they come to me saying they want to lose 5 lbs., I need to work with them to understand what is really driving them at the moment. We need to define their true starting point, and as I have said, it's never about losing 5 lbs. It's all about getting to the real issue, and that is a painful thing for many of my clients. But I let them know that I am not here to judge. I am here to be their guide and hold their hands while we work together to flip the switch and create a new body and life for them. I give them options to set realistic goals, and then we work together to pick the best route for them to achieve their goals. And hey, if we find we get stuck in one intersection, we can make a U-turn and go back to use a different route. You're never stuck unless you stop taking action.

I took a master class with a professional that really helped me. Then I picked a mentor and paid him thousands of dollars to help me get on track and stay my course… and it was worth it. My clients do the same with me. I mean, you can do it by yourself, but it's going to be a lot harder and take a lot longer. So, my clients pay me to be their guide. I say pay, but I don't really like that word. What they really do is invest in themselves to reach their goals. I'm their GPS. I am never the hero of somebody's story. They are the heroes of their own stories. I am just the guide. I'm the one that is hopefully guiding them to their happy ending. Whether it's succeeding at their fitness goals or avoiding pain in their life. Whatever it is, it is my job to help guide them to what makes them successful on their own terms.

So, if you want to achieve your goals, you need to GPS them. First, determine the destination. Then be brutally honest about your realistic location right now at this moment. Then we can determine what you are willing to give or give up to get to your destination as fast as possible; stop yourself from being paralyzed by overthinking. You can always make a U-turn and get back on track. Last but not least, always keep track of where you are, otherwise you might get lost without even knowing it.

" The road to success is not easy to navigate, but with hard work, drive, and passion, it's possible to achieve the American dream."

Tommy Hilfiger

BO'S HOMEWORK

How fast do you want to get to your goal? What's the time frame you give yourself?

_____

_____

_____

_____

What are you willing to give, or give up, to get there faster? Time, money, ego…?

_____

_____

_____

_____

Chapter Eighteen

Everything in the World is an Exchange

When you set your goals, you have the when, the how, the what. Now comes the most important part that is often overlooked. At the bottom of your written goal, you have to add what you are willing to sacrifice for your goal. Because you can never just take away your goals, you can only exchange them for something else. You have to understand what you are willing to give up and exchange for achieving one of these successes or goals or achievements. They are not gifts. If you want to have a higher degree you have to sacrifice years of your life, also lots of your parent's money, or your own future money. If you want to have a ripped, magazine-cover looking body, you have to sacrifice partying, alcohol, eating out, and put in lots of time at the gym. If you want money you have to sacrifice time, or ethics, or stress levels. If you want to have a great relationship you have to make sacrifices too. You get the idea.

Goals, successes, and achievements are not gifts. The first law of thermodynamics, also known as the Law of Conservation of Energy, states that energy can neither be created nor destroyed; energy can only be transferred or changed from one form to another. This means if you want something, you need to be willing to give something in exchange. The one thing that no one ever does but should absolutely do when they write out their goals is to also write out what they are willing to sacrifice to reach them. Is it your health? Is it your time, money, or a relationship? It could sometimes even be your ethics. Would you be willing to sacrifice your ethics to possess something you really want? Interesting question, right? It's not something I recommend, nor would I do it, but there are people who can and do sacrifice ethics to get ahead.

Lots of people say they are willing to go the distance. In my opinion, that is too vague. If you are only willing to go the distance, you're not specific enough. What is the distance anyway? You have to define that. You have to break it down into something way more specific. So, write down one word that describes what you would exchange in order to reach your goal -- one word. For me, that word is **SERVICE**. And service is hard! I am willing to serve, serve, serve... I am a servant, and it may sound fancy, but it's way harder than that. Because a lot of times it takes more time, more money, and extreme mental exhaustion to keep helping others day after day with a smile. And I mean truly helping them and often not expecting anything in return for the extra effort. I am willing to be a servant and not be served in order to reach what I want to achieve in life. By the way, I want you to understand that when I say serve, I don't mean just feeding a hungry person a fish, but rather to feed the person and then teach that person how to fish themself. My methods of helping others are not always fluffy and easy. But I truly want you to succeed in life and not just go to the gym so you can check off a box.

One of the things that I am willing to sacrifice to achieve this is my energy. I'm willing to sacrifice money and give 10 years of my life to reach my own dream. It's a very simple principle for me. When I first started going into business, I knew it would take money. I had to make a very difficult decision. I knew I had my family to support, and I was thinking of starting something I didn't even know would work out. I didn't know anyone in the industry who would help me, and I felt like a blind person trying to cross a highway. There is so much competition in the gym world, and it felt like everyone was out to get me. I felt like I was the lone wolf.

Obviously, starting a business takes some money, and I had a little bit of money saved up. But I had to make a decision on whether I should pursue my dream or use the money for other purposes. I had a wife and two kids to support. I had to decide whether I would use the money to buy a bigger car for my family and get a better place to live or invest it in a business having no idea whether it would work or not. It was a very, very hard decision for me to make. To this day, my wife is driving a very small, very old Honda Fit that is starting to rust and fall apart. It was a salvage car I got and fixed up about 5 years ago. My whole family has to fit in that car. And I couldn't buy a van, because I needed to invest the little amount of money I had into a business I wasn't sure would make it.

When I first started my business, the four of us lived in a one-bedroom apartment. All was invested in the fitness studio I was about to open. This was my sacrifice. A year later, we were actually able to move into a bigger apartment. We lived in a pretty questionable neighborhood. Instead of investing in a house for the family, we had to live in a bad neighborhood while I built a business. I'm talking about a place where there were cracks in the walls, and the neighbors were loud all the time. Yet I selfishly invested the money into the business. Now it would be selfish of me to make this decision on my own, so I sat down with my family and wife and laid out all the options. I told them I could stick with my current job, and we could get a little better house; maybe get a better car. Or invest in this unknown and see if I could make a go of it. I talked with my wife and told her that she deserved the best, and I would not take that away from my family in order to achieve my own ambitious goals if we all didn't agree. Well, she told me she knew that my goals were ambitious and selfish, but she also knew how much I wanted to be able to help others. She assured me that at some point, the money would come as a side effect of helping others, and we would all be just fine. There she was telling me to do it. Holy crap! I was like, you are the most beautiful person in the world. And believe me, she is. She is my strength, my everything!

I am a few years into this business now, and we are still living in a kind of questionable neighborhood. The car has dents because the neighbors open their doors into it. And the neighbor kids walk around throwing apples and rocks at it for some reason. But I am helping others with my business. I am changing lives, and that is what I want to do. I'm still not making much money from the business because I continuously re-invest it, but the business is growing. I'm only 31, and my wife supports me completely. I have a wonderful family. To be very clear, I did not give up a good lifestyle for my family, what I gave up was having this conversation with my wife and asking her to allow me to make us a little uncomfortable to pursue my dreams and goals. That conversation is what I was willing to sacrifice. And that was one of the hardest sacrifices I have ever had to make in my life!

I feel being vulnerable in front of my wife is harder than being vulnerable with other people. After all, I'm supposed to be my wife's and family's rock, their armor. I'm the knight that is supposed to defend my castle, but sometimes I have to be vulnerable in front of her. Sometimes I feel she has more strength than I will ever have. You know that I'm just an immigrant. I don't have much money, and the little money we have had has been invested in my dream of being able to help people. But it is also my dream to change so many people's lives for the better through my business, through my trainers, through my books, through my work and through any means necessary, that eventually, my family will have the financial freedom and abundance they deserve.

Unfortunately, to run a successful business, you need to know sales. When you know sales, you know how to talk to people in a smart way. I talk to people very casually to gain information from them. For people out there that are putting off changing their health and life, I mean this next thought in the sincerest way. In my previous jobs, I was taught to approach sales as a way of getting people to buy my stuff. But I realized that the reason I really wanted the information was to get to know them better so that I could serve and help them most effectively. Sadly, many of them will tell me that they can't afford the training, but then I see their posts on social media with photos of all the partying they did over the weekend and the new clothes they bought themselves or even restaurants they visit weekly. This shows me that they did have the money but chose to invest it in frivolous things instead of investing in themselves and their health. It boggles my mind. Not to mention that partying and eating out is what made them approach a trainer in the first place. I truly don't understand it.

So then, how bad do you want it? If this cookie, this drink, or this lifestyle is more important to you than being healthy and fit, I am not going to judge you. I'm just here to let you know the path you're headed down is not a good one. If you lie to yourself and tell yourself that you don't have the money for a trainer, a doctor, or a nutritionist, or a counselor, but you have it to spend on the latest smartphones and partying, that is up to you. But I will tell you that this self-destructive behavior will catch up to you in the long run. This is not a scare tactic to get you to buy my services. You could be a thousand miles away from my studio reading this book. It's all about what you want in life and how badly you want it.

You are the keeper of your dreams, and you are the master of achieving them. Just know that whatever you decide, you are only trading one for the other because everything we do in this world is an exchange. So, what are you willing to sacrifice in order to achieve your goals or dreams?

"Great achievement is usually born of great sacrifice, and is never the result of selfishness ."

Napoleon Hill

BO'S HOMEWORK

Are you willing to invest in you?

_____

_____

_____

_____

Are you willing to sacrifice temporary pleasure for longevity
and long-lasting happiness?

_____

_____

_____

_____

Chapter Nineteen

Make Quick Decisions

Most people get caught up in this analysis-paralysis I have already talked about. It is extremely difficult to make decisions that carry the kind of responsibility as those that impact your business. It is very challenging to take responsibility for your decisions. It makes you vulnerable. It makes you hurt, and it can even hurt other people.

Sometimes decisions will cost you. Making the wrong decision can have tough consequences. The outcome may be bad and cost you, but you will always learn very important lessons from it. If you don't make a decision, you will lose out by default. An opportunity you may have had will evaporate, and the consequences from that can be just as bad as making

167

the wrong decision. How many times have you heard people say that they wished they would have done something but never made the decision to do it? We almost never regret a decision we made, but we often regret the ones we never made. Back when I was working in home healthcare as a personal care assistant, I've heard many people at the end of their lives talk about the things they regretted not doing. I rarely ever heard them talk about regretting the things that they did. If you go for something and it's not working out, you can always make a U-turn and put yourself back on track. The key is to not let it overtake you and to learn from the mistake or error. At this point, you haven't lost a lot except maybe some time, and you can keep on going.

Habits are a muscle you can train. You can train yourself to have good habits or bad habits. I see this all the time. It's the same thing with decisions. You can train yourself to be more decisive and respond more quickly to things. It's like turning your consciousness on to look at things more clearly and snap you back to reality when you need it. Everything is built on repetition. So, developing decision-making skills is like training for anything else, the more you do it, the better you are going to get at it.

When you make a decision, there is a consequence. If it doesn't go well or make sense, you're going to learn a lesson from it. If it's right and works out, you're going to build your confidence. No matter what happens, you will either have to work through it and apply that lesson next time, or you win and celebrate!

If somebody asks you to play a game and you don't want to lose, you may tell them you don't want to play. But to me, you just lost. You didn't even try, so they win automatically. You might be afraid to play because you don't want to lose, but I play to win. Look, you don't really want to be that kid stuck in the back of the room watching everyone else play. Take a risk and join the game. What have you got to lose? At the very least, you will have learned how to play the game. And you might even find that you're good at it and you like it! Maybe it won't work out. But maybe seeing if it does will be the best adventure ever!?

When you are a businessman who has control of your own life, you know that sometimes things just don't go your way. But if you never make a decision, you gain nothing. In order to become stronger in anything that you do, you have to be willing to bring yourself to the point of failure if necessary. It's the only way for you to grow and learn. If you're not sore at the end of the day, then you didn't push yourself hard enough. When you ride your bicycle, the more resistance you feel in your legs and the pedals, the faster you're going, the further you are, the more you will see, the stronger your legs will become. If you're squatting or bench pressing, the stronger the resistance to the bar while lowering it, the stronger you are. Strength is measured by resistance against you. Character is measured by resilience. Endurance is measured by a pain threshold. Business is measured by problem-solving. Absolutely anything great in life is measured by your ability to overcome discomfort, pain, and problems.

Leave no room for interpretation. Make a decision, or the decision will be made for you! If you have a hard time making decisions, make the commitment. Usually, that means laying down the money. Then you have no choice, right? When you put money down you just put value on it. So, now you have to follow through because you put your money where your mouth is. I've done this many times, and it is a good motivator. There is no guarantee it will work, but I know that I will learn something, whether I fail or succeed. So, it has value because I put my money on it and value because I will get something out of it no matter what!

Here is a good example of quick decision making. And it's kind of funny. With the business, the last seven years, I've had no vacation that was more than 3 days long. As you may guess, I have a hard time leaving the business. There is always something that needs my attention. And yes, I'm finally starting to hire people that I can trust to be there, but it's still a challenge. I kept on promising my family that we will be going on a vacation. But of course, something always comes up with the business. So, one day, like so many other days, I called my wife and let her know I would be late again because I had signed up two new clients. She was very understanding as always, and then a minute later, she sent me a picture of my kids sleeping, and I knew that I would not get to see them that night. This hit me hard right in the gut! So, I made a snap decision to go someplace that very weekend. I got on my phone and immediately booked hotels for us, and we went. The best thing was that I came back to the business refreshed and even stronger.

So, make a quick decision. If it's a small decision, then make a quick mental list of pros and cons. If it's a big decision then sleep on it for a night or two. But then you have to give a firm Yes or No and move on with your life without looking back. The only thing you are allowed to keep is the lesson. If you wait around to try to justify or analyze every angle, you'll miss out. And that is the formula for getting stuck. Quick decisions create action, and action carries momentum to keep propelling you forward. If the decision falls short, make a U-turn and learn from it so you can take yourself forward again. Remember, the more decisive you are, the better you will become at it.

"Decision is a sharp knife that cuts clean and straight; indecision, a dull one that hacks and tears and leaves ragged edges behind it."

Gordon Graham

BO'S HOMEWORK

Are you decisive?

_____

_____

_____

_____

What happens when you realize the decision you made may not have been the right one?

_____

_____

_____

_____

What is the hardest decision you've ever made so far?

_____

_____

_____

_____

Chapter Twenty

Give, and It Will be Given to You

Luke 6:38 – Give, and it will be given to you. You cannot create anything. It has always existed. Everything is an exchange. If you try to make quick money by lying to people and taking advantage of them, it's going to come back on you in the end. It's kind of like the karma thing. If you keep giving, I believe that you will eventually receive. This is something that I live by. If you don't do the right thing, it's going to come back to bite you in some way. You know when you are not living up to your own standards.

I live by serving and giving. My goal is not to be rich. Rather, my goal is to be successful. To me, success is being healthy. Success is strong mentally, physically and spiritually.

Success is financially and ideologically free. Success is having my family next to me and changing lives for a living. I don't have a lot, but never in my life have I felt like I didn't have enough. I can honestly say that I have nothing to complain about. I mean just look around. I have my family, and they love me. I get to change and improve lives for a living. And most importantly, I have my consciousness. I do not do any drugs. I never drink; not even beer, I don't like it. I try to not do anything that could potentially take control of my mind and influence my ability to make a decision that doesn't align with my rationale and heart.

I have nothing to complain about in this life. Every decision I make is my own. Nobody makes me work 25 hours a day. I choose to do this. I am doing my best to do things right. When I go to sleep at night I usually don't sleep well because my anxiety kicks in and I start to worry about all the problems I have to solve, people I want to help, decisions I have to make and goals I want to achieve. But what I can tell you is that I have peace of mind knowing the decisions I have made so far in life have caused few mistakes and failures. And although I have had failures, and they've been very painful sometimes, they have made me who I am today. The wrinkles that I am starting to have on my face show that I am smiling a lot. The gray hairs on my sideburns and the receding hairline show that I truly care. And all my injuries and scars show that I am living life to the fullest.

      I have a code I live by that I am always trying to live up to. I am trying to live my life so that people know they can count on my word. My name is my word, and my word is gold. I will do whatever is in my power to honor my word. That is what I want my legacy to be. When people speak or hear my name, I want them to know that I always delivered on my word, or at the very least, did everything in my power to do so. I am far from being perfect, but I am working every day and trying to become a better version of myself.

      I will continue to serve and help. The best way to make a change is by example. I know I will stumble and sometimes even fall, but I will try my absolute best. I want to make this world a better place! One workout at a time. One conversation at a time. One book at a time. One smile at a time. One changed life at a time. This journey is not going to be easy, but it will be the most fulfilling adventure of my life! Are you coming with me? Then Stay Sore!

THANK YOU FOR READING MY BOOK!

Being vulnerable and sharing events of your life publicly is not something that comes easy. It is my sincere hope that you found Stay Sore valuable and that you may share this book with another individual. If this book has motivated you, inspired you, or even just challenged your thinking patterns, I have already accomplished my mission. Thank you for picking up my book and investing your time reading my story. I deeply appreciate it.

I would also like to thank a few very special people in my life. I want to thank my parents for teaching me to always try to do the right thing, despite crippling fear, anxiety, doubt, or the chance of being judged. I want to thank my best friend and wife, Kate, for always supporting me, no matter how crazy, unrealistic or ambitious my ideas are. I also want to thank my two boys and my future third baby boy, with whom my wife is pregnant right now, for giving me the motivation and inspiration to be a better role model and to try even harder. I want to thank all my clients over the last decade that I have been in the fitness industry. You probably don't realize it, but by trusting me with your time, body and mind – you give me purpose! And most importantly, I want to thank God for

STAY SORE

creating this body, mind, and soul of mine and being patient with me while I'm trying to figure this thing out.

Thank you and Stay Sore.

Your favorite trainer,
Bo.

Follow me on Instagram and Facebook

@bo_skitsko

#StaySore

You can also contact me at

boskitsko@gmail.com

And make sure to check out my gym Bo-Fit

www.bofitstudio.com
@bofitstudio

Made in the USA
Middletown, DE
12 January 2020